KNOWING

SHAWNA ALLARD

ZANDER

Livonia, Michigan

KNOWING

Published by Zander
an imprint of BHC Press

Library of Congress Control Number:
2017945136

ISBN-13: 978-1-946848-50-5
ISBN-10: 1-946848-50-6

Visit the publisher at:
www.bhcpress.com

Also available in ebook

ACKNOWLEDGMENTS

To Divine Creator, the loving source that permeates all that is—including this book.

The true love of my life, Peter Allard, for listening (a lot), editing, and all of your support in more ways than I can count. You still make me laugh :)

To Mom for always encouraging me to be my best self and for all the fun and confidences we share. You are a true friend "a belle and a confidante."

To my precious children who have been my "Why" in life and my teachers.

Thank you Poppy for your wise counsel and guidance.

I am gratefully surrounded and blessed with special soul sisters on my path, and each has inspired a special part in me and in this book. Thank you to my "Book Club" Goddess Group, Mary Odgers, Nancy Ruggles, Kim Nadel, Jolene Priesto, and Marcela Alva.

I am grateful to my soul sister Melanie Lococo for that final push forward.

Thank you to Tracie Hassie, Tracey Shoman, Judy and Ken Foster, Jill Silverman, Sue Duclose Snyder, Christina Hills, Valerie Sorrentino.

Thank you Juliette Sobanet, my author friend and mentor. Your guidance made all the difference.

I am grateful to my photographer and dear friend Michelle Hawker for a fun photo shoot and the photo on the back cover.

Thank you Alicia at iProofread And More for editing this book.

Thank you to Vern and Joni, my publishers at BHC Press.

Thank you to my Literary Agent Ariela Wilcox without whom this book would still be a maybe.

Thank you Nancy Williamson for your wise counsel, friendship, and mentoring.

To Paramahansa Yogananda for wisdom, awakening, and so much, much more.

I am deeply grateful for the love and support of my family and my family of friends.

Most importantly to my clients for sharing your questions and your seeking hearts over the last three decades.

TABLE OF CONTENTS

AUTHOR'S NOTE

DEDICATION

To God and to my family.
I am who I am because of you.

To my husband, Peter Allard,
for your love, patience, guidance and faith
in me when I had none in myself.

To my children Casey, Jenna, and Michael.
Each of you are so uniquely special and
I love you more deeply than words can convey.

To my mom, Jenny Chopak,
you are a "Belle and a Confidant."

I will love each of you,
through all of our lifetimes,
until the end of time.

ENJOYING FREEDOM
OF RELIGIOUS BELIEFS

Ideally we can all enjoy freedom of religious beliefs. My work, my being, and the entire reason for my existence is to celebrate our Creator whom I refer to as Divine, Source, Spirit or God. I use several words to mean God. In every case I am referring to a single source of creation in the universe. Please use whatever name suits you best in describing the Omnipresent energy of the Creator. My intention is to not impress any specific religious belief on anyone. This book comes from the Knowledge that we are all one. Each of us needs to find our own unique path to spiritual awakening.

THE BEGINNING

You are about to share an intimate experience with me about my life as an intuitive channel. I was born to be an intuitive channel and though it has always been my destiny, it took many years for me to embrace or even understand it. For many years I was reluctant to be different and misunderstood or worse yet judged. I often experienced prejudice if I shared the truth of my Gift. I just wanted to fit in and be liked. It took 30 years of my life to grow into my 'Calling' and it is now another 30 years since then. I have learned to own and embrace my unique gift as an intuitive channel. Divine has an extraordinary way of speaking through me to bring clarity and divine insights to seekers. In these pages you will glimpse insightful messages that my clients have received during readings. I will show you practical ways in which you can learn to awaken and know your own unique intuitive voice. You will learn how to tap into life's greatest wellspring of knowledge and '**know what you need to know**'.

If you have ever suffered the pain of indecision around relationships, parenting, health, or career this book is designed to help you. It can be very debilitating when you simply do not know where to turn and what to do. We all have intuitive abilities and learning to develop and understand your personal intuitive voice is profoundly helpful. You will receive guidance through the questions, answers, and experiences I and my clients have had over my 30 years as an intuitive counselor.

This is an inspirational journey including insightful dialogue with Divine and this book is filled with practical life lessons. Explore proven methods to awaken your personal intuitive voice. Gain hope and peace when you read the insights others have received during sessions with Spirit.

I am now enjoying a very joyful and rewarding life filled with love, peace, and joy. I celebrate a full and rewarding practice as a professional intuitive consultant, financial stability and the love of friends and family, but it wasn't always that way.

I was the firstborn to a young couple just barely twenty-one, married right out of high school, this being the norm in the early 1950's. I was loved, cared for, and nurtured.

Still, on October 30th, 1958 something tragic happened and I was never the same again.

My dad is a 24 year old, still a kid himself really, who sees no problem in leaving me with his parents so he can attend a Halloween party.

My mom is in the hospital. I am two years and five months old and my baby brother is being born tonight.

I am spending the night at my grandparents' house. I am snuggled under the covers clutching my favorite dingy and once white blanket. I have the satin border to my nose for the comfort of its familiar smell and touch. The smell and touch of my blanket is indescribably delicious. It is the very smell and feel of home, love, and comfort.

Something is disturbing my sleep and for a moment I'm not sure where I am. Oh yeah, I realize I am at Grandma and Grandpa's house.

The room is filled with a chilling darkness that makes me feel very uncomfortable and scared. Then I realized he is sitting on my bed.

I'm feeling frightened of him so I get out of bed and wander into the hallway; then I move into the front room. The darkness throughout the house terrifies me, and there is a little more light in the front room. He isn't picking me up to carry me. He is just following me. I don't know where to go to get away from him. I am barefoot and the floor is cold against my feet. I want my mommy and daddy.

I am wearing my favorite frilly little girl nightie. The fabric has two layers of nylon ruffles, pale pink with a tiny purple rosebud sewn to the lace on the front.

I am very cold and confused. I see a spot where the streetlight is coming through the drapes and I move towards the light. I lie down on the carpet in the sliver of light, clutching my faithful blanket.

I am cold, frightened, and crying. He is bending over me. His mustache is scratchy and I don't like how he smells. He is persistent even as I wiggle away. He is really hurting me and I want him to leave me alone. He tells me that I must never tell my parents about how bad I have been or anything about this secret. I am not sure of his exact words now, but I do know that if I tell anyone anything, my mommy and daddy will die. Then I will have to live here with him forever and ever. I am whimpering for my mommy and daddy. I am lost in terror. I am holding my breath afraid to breathe or scream.

In my next awareness, I have left my body and I am hovering at the ceiling with angels. I feel completely loved and safe. I am warm and at peace. I look down and say to the angels, "Oh no, I think that little baby is going to die." Immediately upon my recognition and statement, I am back in my body again.

The following morning I am terribly upset and crying. My grandmother, trying to comfort me, gives me a Werther's hard candy, butterscotch flavor. My memory is so vivid of the dresser drawer she

THE BEGINNING

retrieved them from, the crinkle of the bag, and oh, the smell of being rescued by butterscotch. I wish the recovery process from incest was as simple as butterscotch candy.

When my parents come to pick me up I am inconsolable. All I can tell my mom is, "I called you and called you, but you didn't come."

I was molested by my grandfather when I was two and a half. It was on this night when I first experienced leaving my body and joining the angels on the ceiling.

I was a talker. Some say I talked on my way out of the womb. I was a bossy little girl as well. Deciding the rules of games while playing with other children, I think there were times I changed the rules along the way to suit me. When my baby brother came home from the hospital I was excited to be a young super hero (side kick to my Super Mom) bringing diapers and helping in any way that I could. I was equally as excited when my little sister was born a few years later. I knew since the beginning of time that I would be a mom. I saw a vision of my first two children long before I was pregnant with them. I "knew" them in Spirit. This was more than a longing for them—it was an eventuality that I looked forward to. I also "knew" a third child that was represented to me as a twinkling star whenever I spoke with the first two souls. I knew this third child would be born a bit later in time, after the first two. As I understood, this child would be chosen later.

God bless my mom for all the listening she did. I followed her around talking all the time. I later understood that my brother and sister felt I dominated her time. I am very sorry about that. However, at the time no one knew it was a compulsion, led by anxiety and a trauma I could not talk about, or resolve.

I had terrible nightmares often of the same man chasing me and I could not scream. I had a special bedtime routine some might describe as OCD. I wore my "special" safe pajamas, wound my alarm clock and rechecked it a few times, even getting out of bed to recheck that it was wound. I did twenty sit-ups each night before bed and could not sleep if I didn't do these. I liked my sheets with the roses on them. The design faced outward so that the thorns would protect me.

I was a very emotionally sensitive child. I was sensitive in other ways as well. I could not bear the high-pitched whine in my head when I walked near a jewelry store or men's clothing store, as they had alarm systems. I could hear and feel the alarms, even though others could not. A physical pain hurt my ears and head so terribly if I walked near them.

I was eager to please and be good. I was never, ever wanting to break the rules. I couldn't stand to have someone mad at me.

I loved our Methodist church. As well as attending regularly, I volunteered to help in Sunday school classes for younger children and went to Bible study during the week. I was baptized at thirteen after attending our church education classes. I loved the singing part a lot and joined the choir.

Singing brought me great peace and joy. I also loved singing while I was waterskiing. I would sing out loud with a heart full of love and adventure as I was waterskiing with the vast openness of nature all around, and with the spray of the water hitting my face. I only ever sang one song while waterskiing, and that was an old country song: "The Happiest Girl in the Whole USA" sung by Donna Fargo.

A few unusual things happened that began to indicate my gift of intuition. When I was nine years old I was listening to the adults in my family talking. My Uncle Ron was talking about a book he was reading about Semyon Kirlian and his discovery of Kirlian photography. He explained that we all have an energy field around us and plants and every living thing have an energy field. Kirlian photography was a discovery that was able to capture this energy field in a photograph. He also mentioned that "some people can actually see colors and light around people." At that moment I realized I was "some people" and I really didn't think that sounded good. I felt I needed to be sure what made a person "some people" and if that was an okay thing to be. I also needed to confirm if I was in fact "some people." I asked Uncle Ron if he was referring to the yellow glow around his head. He got very excited as did the other adults, and I proceeded to tell everyone the color of the light that surrounded them.

Sometime later when I was about eleven years old I went to a weekend Bible Camp. When I would pray, sometimes I would feel a special feeling of warmth and elevation, feeling very light almost as if the room would lift away and I was with the angels again. This happened one evening at Bible Camp and I was suddenly aware of people gathered around me saying, "Shawna spoke in Tongues!" (I didn't know what that meant.) I was deeply moved and crying, not sad, just moved to tears from the overwhelming experience I had just been through. Spirit had spoken through me while I was in an unconscious state. I was embarrassed by all the fuss and attention given to me after that.

I was a Camp Fire girl (similar to Girl Scouts) when I was in grammar school. Before a trip by train up to Santa Barbara, California, I became quite concerned and consumed with worry that the train would jump the tracks. Much assurance was given that it would not and could not happen and I should not worry. Eventually I followed their advice and boarded the train. We did make it to Santa Barbara just fine and had a great day. As the train was returning to bring us home, and before it arrived at the station to pick us up in Santa Barbara, it jumped the tracks. We were all bussed back home to La Crescenta, California.

My parents were totally open to me attending different churches with friends, so I had many opportunities to attend Catholic mass,

Synagogue, and various new age churches as well. I have always had an open mind and found religions interesting.

I remember our avocado green rotary-dial wall phone that hung on the wall in our kitchen. In early December of 1971 as we arrived home from a Christmas shopping trip at the mall, the phone was ringing. It felt to me like the whole world froze into place as my mother answered the phone. I KNEW what I could not comprehend. My dad was in a catastrophic car accident. I was fifteen when my dad became paralyzed from the neck down. I heard the word quadriplegic for the first time. He had been in Mammoth, a mountainous skiing area in California, at the time and the truck he was in slid on ice and crashed. He broke his neck at the fourth and fifth vertebrae. Mom flew up immediately to be with Dad. She wanted to protect us from the most gruesome parts and we would have to wait to visit him until he was more stabilized. We stayed with family friends and continued to attend school.

On Christmas Eve my dad's condition was getting worse and he was looking as if he might not live. My thirteen-year-old brother, ten-year-old sister and I boarded a plane for Reno, Nevada, where Dad was in the hospital. It was a small plane and a bumpy ride in very stormy conditions. It was a flight right out of a scary movie with all of us tightly strapped in and with many passengers clutching air sick bags. It was just the three of us children, on our first flight alone, and we were all motion sick and terrified. Mom met us at the airport in Reno.

It may sound unusual with all that was happening, but waking in Reno in the morning to a blanket of undisturbed snow seemed surreal and magical. We were up before the dawn and, as we walked out to a world covered in glistening snow, we were making the first footprints in this pristine white and silent morning. We were captivated by the long hanging icicles. We walked to the hospital in the snow and the four of us had a very special closeness. The world was soundless around us because of the deep snowstorm. This would become one of my most special Christmas memories. No gifts, no tree or special feast, just the intimacy of our family togetherness at my dad's side. Children were only allowed in hospitals in 1971 if a family member was near death. As we entered my dad's hospital room nothing could have prepared me for the sights and sounds of what I would see and feel. My dad, who had always been extremely fit and strong, was now strapped to a platform, bolts drilled into his shaved head, and he was barely talking. I prayed fervently for God to heal him so that he could walk again.

Years and years of prayers produced no change. It was more than a dozen years later before I understood karma, or the spiritual lessons that all of us come to Earth to learn and the relevance that could be why someone might suffer. I still kept up my prayers and often woke from dreams of my dad walking again. I do not know why that was his path and consequently the path for my family as well. He lived in and out of the hospital as a quadriplegic for the next twenty-seven years.

My dad was moved to the Veterans' Administration Hospital in Long Beach, California, about four hours from our home. After making the drive every weekend for several months in a row, we became very weary. My mom decided it was time to move closer to where he would be for a long time, possibly forever. We moved to Orange County, California, when I was a junior in high school. I attended El Modena High School and graduated in 1974. In the Fall of 1974 I went to Brooks College and received a degree in Fashion Design.

I was a fashion designer for a few years, and while it was exciting and fulfilling on a creative level, the culture and city life of the Los Angeles fashion industry were not for me. Intuition told me to move to Vail, Colorado, and reassess my career of choice.

I arrived in Vail, Colorado, just in time for spring skiing in March of 1978 with a plan to stay one year. I loved Vail and the beautiful mountains and all the athletic young people I met. I found employment as a waitress at The Lodge At Vail fine dining room. I would ski all day, and ski right into the spa at The Lodge At Vail for a shower before work. I waited tables from six to midnight, and then I had just enough time to dance at a local hot spot. The next day I did it all again. Vail Village had a demographic at that time of about five to one, men to women, and this rose much higher during the ski season. This worked quite well for me and I often had a ski date and dinner date on the same day. I was never in need of a dance partner and all the men and women shared my love of nature and adventure.

When the snow melted I went hiking every chance I got. Nature was my place of worship and filled me with God's blessings. I took up mountain biking and loved that too. Life in Vail suited me completely.

In September of 1982 with the ski season quickly approaching, all I could think about was the excitement of the coming season. I had always received a season ski pass as part of my work compensation, as was customary for ski resort employees. This year my employer was not providing season ski passes, and I could not afford the annual price. I came up with a solution to this problem and I decided to run for Miss Vail Colorado. If I won, one of my prizes would include a season ski pass! The competition lasted for one week. Fifteen women competed and the contest included the usual beauty pageant events like speaking and poise. I won! I won the title of Miss Vail Colorado 1982-83 along with my season ski pass and many very cool prizes. The coming year was filled with many exciting experiences.

In December of that year I introduced President and Mrs. Ford at our Tree Lighting event and sang Christmas carols with them. Professional golfer Jack Nicklaus, helped me through the snowy streets in my high heels and up onto the stage. He was very nice. During that year I spoke at or attended many social functions. I helped with the Ford Golf Championship. I volunteered for various charities, concerts, and events as well as sat on the events planning committee for the Town of Vail.

Then I moved on to the position of Vail Ambassador, as a member of the Vail Ambassador's club, where I served the Vail community alongside former Miss Vail Colorado winners. We helped with events like the World Alpine Ski Championships in 1989. I met a lot of actors, actresses, and other famous people during this time. I don't remember who, really, except for Bob Hope, Clint Eastwood, and all of Charlie's Angels, as well as many dignitaries from around the world.

I fell in love and married at thirty years old. We were partners in the Vail Management Company and I was our accountant.

In August of 1988 we had our first child, a baby boy. I was a very happy mother. I had known both of my children in Spirit for many years. I knew my son would be blond with blue eyes even though his father and I had darker hair and eyes. I knew my daughter-to-be would have my coloring and even look like me.

My husband did not enjoy being a family man, and as a result began to withdraw and become very distant. He resented the fact that motherhood took up so much of my time. I knew he didn't want any more children and I also knew I was meant to have my little girl. I prayed vigilantly to God, and pleaded for my own dreams to come true. Night after night I went to sleep with the prayer of a second baby, my little girl. One night, however, I was struck by the thought that if my husband was a man to pray, his prayer would be the opposite from mine. He would be praying for us not to have another baby. I realized how wrong I was to pray to God for my selfish wish and that God was the same God for all. That night I offered to God that I would never again ask for anything for myself but rather that God guide us to what was best for all. I surrendered to God and that his will be done, for the highest and best good of our entire family. I was awake that night crying and mourning my baby girl. My grief was deep and crushing as it is when you lose a child.

The next day, despite birth control, I became pregnant with my daughter.

Two weeks later when the pregnancy test confirmed her conception it was Valentine's Day. I was overcome with joy and elation. I delivered the news of our coming baby, and in return, I was delivered quite a blow. My husband let me know that in today's world I had options that would solve this "problem" and I needed to make a decision. To which I said, "She stays and you are the only one here with a choice to make." He did stay until shortly after our baby was born, but he was distant, mean, and cold. He loved his daughter when she arrived and our son as well. I was hopeful for our family, and our marriage.

Before our daughter was born, I had daily conversations with this beautiful soul. In our conversations she was not a baby at all. She was a tall, slender angelic being. We had been close in many other lifetimes before this one. She told me many things. One of which was that her name had been Christina with her nickname which was Kaitlin. However, I chose not to name her Christina or Kaitlin. As a young girl between the age of three and five my daughter referred to herself as Kaitlin. I have gifts she made for me during these years that are signed, "I love you, Mommy, Kaitlin Jenna."

A week or two into my pregnancy I was visited by the Holy Spirit. A light so bright and intense that I could not move. I was consumed with a loving presence that permeated my being beyond any earthly love I have ever known. I was literally bathed in the most wonderful presence of love and light. I have a bit of reluctance to admit that I was scared, but I was scared and overwhelmed. It is too intimate to share what the Angel said at this time, but I must say that it changed my life and my level of intuition forever more.

I had a daily practice of meditation and prayer at 11:30 a.m. while my babies were napping.

One day Spirit said get tarot cards. I felt so very foolish going into a store and asking to buy tarot cards. I was imagining someone saying "what qualifications do you have?" or "who do you think you are buying those?" or "what makes you think you have any right to those?" There were three choices of tarot cards. I chose the deck that felt right and I also purchased a book that would explain how to lay out the cards, as well as the meaning of each card.

During my usual meditation and spiritual time I sat down to study my book. First the phone rang, and then the door bell, and then the door bell rang again and again. My dog got out and then my baby woke up from an unusually short nap. A neighbor needed my help with something, and my study time was ruined. I sat down frustrated and just asked, "What? Why?" Spirit answered: **"Do not study...just read...it is just a tool for practice...no rules."** I proceeded to shuffle and practice for a few days. While I was shuffling the cards, I was also praying, and breathing very deeply. My eyes were closed and focused on the third eye. Soon I found that even in preparation for reading the cards a shift was happening within me. I would enter a trance and sometime later I would awaken to find cards spilled to my lap and the floor. I felt like I knew a bunch of information but it was now just out of reach, as if a dream I couldn't quite recall.

Spirit said: **"Automatic Writing"** so I bought a spiral notebook and kept a daily journal of anything Spirit would say to me during meditation or my trance state. I would write, or scribble really, so as not to leave the trance. After my meditation was over I would read the words I had written. I was actually amazed at how wise and intuitive they seemed to be. I was instructed to write anything that felt directed to me from Spirit and not to judge or censor in any way.

One day I asked, "Dear God, what would you have me do? How can I best serve thy will, while being a good mother and providing for my children? I certainly did not expect the answer to be...

"Telegraphing!"

I grew up with intuitive knowing. This time it was not an intuitive knowing, but rather a booming voice inside of my head and there was no doubt about it! It was loud enough that I felt the neighbors could hear it.

I freaked out! I grabbed the baby monitor and ran around and around the exterior of my home with the baby monitor clutched to my breast. I ran while thinking, "What just happened in there?" I ran until I was exhausted and calm enough to realize I had been praying and asked God for guidance.

I sat to meditate again and asked, or rather demanded, *"Who is this?"*

The answer came as a huge movement of love through my entire body as I had only experienced before when visited by The Holy Spirit during my second pregnancy. The answer was simply: **"Who did you call?"** I knew in the depths of my soul that I was in God's hands. I asked, "Telegraphing? Really? Like should I work for the phone company?" The answer came immediately.

"No! Telegraphing: the process of communicating from one source to another through a conduit. WE CAN SPEAK THROUGH YOU IF YOU WILL ALLOW IT!"

Some days passed as I digested this new reality. I agreed and said to Spirit, "Please help me to trust my intuition and give me clarity that this is all real. I don't doubt you, but I very much doubt myself at this moment."

Below are some examples of just a few of the strange things I would be writing down during my sessions with Divine. Once I wrote the strangest word that meant nothing to me as I phonetically

THE BEGINNING

scrawled it out. The word turned out to be the name of the prescription I would be picking up for my mother in-law later that day.

Divine would say "light bulb" and sure enough a light bulb would blow as I turned on the bathroom light just moments later.

A great example was the day Divine said, **"Your husband will purchase a new red car today."** My thought was that he surely better not. And besides, I thought, it wouldn't even be possible. There are no dealerships in Vail, Colorado; he would have to travel through the snowy mountain roads for over two hours to Denver, and he is working today, and we have NEVER talked at all about this!! A few hours later he arrived in our driveway with a brand new apple red Subaru.

I continued to meditate at 11:30 a.m. every day until the babies woke from their naps. I also continued to receive from Spirit, lessons, guidance, and assurance of this intuitive accountability.

One afternoon, much to my amazement, I received a "Download" of information for my brother who lived in California. I had not told him, or anyone for that matter, what was going on. I felt very awkward about this information. I was sure I would be judged, and not in a good way. Still, I had information that did not belong to me. It came through me in service for another person. If I kept the information that was meant for someone else, I would be wrong. If I didn't share it then I felt out of order for possessing knowledge that belonged to someone else. It felt somewhat like finding an item of value and wanting to return it, but wondering if you would be then accused of stealing it.

I did call my brother and share the information with him. He was very understanding and even shared some of his experiences where his own intuition had helped him. He was grateful for the reading, saying that it was accurate, pertinent, and useful for exactly what he was dealing with.

The following day he asked me if a secretary downstairs from his office could give me a call. Shortly after that I read for the secretary's mother and my sister-in-law as well. Word got around, and I began doing a reading a day free of charge to whomever called me at 11:30 a.m. I did not ask for money but I did request confirmation as to the accuracy and helpfulness of what I was offering.

One evening I was visiting my neighbor while our children played. The phone rang and I immediately knew it was about a job for her husband. I knew what he should wear to the interview, and many other details. Although I felt very foolish and even out of line for intruding in such a way, I shared the information with her. It turned out to be an accurate description of those who would interview him as well as other knowledge he needed for the interview. He got the job!

After this incident I felt Divine Spirit and I needed to talk about some boundaries. I explained, "I would not want a neighbor knowing something about me I had not invited them to share in. It feels like it's snooping and it feels wrong. I don't ever want to know anything again unless someone invites me and asks for assistance. Then by all means bring it on!"

My belief has always been that I am meditating several times a day and if there is anything I should know, Divine Spirit certainly knows how to reach me. I do readings for myself sometimes by having a family member ask the questions as I channel the answers. I trust in Divine, that I will "Know What I Need to Know."

Many months of not charging went on and then Spirit told me to charge twenty-five dollars. I was not excited, but nervous because I was afraid no one would call if I had to charge them. I was actually addicted to reading for people. If ever a day came when no one would call for a reading, I would call my mom or sister to ask if I could please read for them.

A year or so later I was told to raise my prices to forty-five dollars. I was reluctant to do this for fear the value wasn't there and out of fear that no one would pay the higher price. I kept my prices the same. All calls stopped and no one requested a reading. I went a week without receiving any requests for readings. Not one call at all for a reading. When I asked Divine Spirit why, the answer made sense. **"If you will not listen and trust our guidance to raise your price, how can you expect anyone else to listen?"** I said that I would charge the new fee on the very next phone call and the phone began immediately to ring! Another call for a reading came through right after that one.

Shortly after this I became a single mother of two toddlers. My spouse was an angry man and purposely left us without a credit card, checkbook, or source of income. He did not pay child support, and one evening at 9:30 p.m. he sent a tow truck to my house to repossess the red Subaru. It was a miserable and trying time, to say the least. There was much more drama, which I will spare you here. I do call it my Near Death Divorce for a reason. It does seem a wonder I came back to life after that time.

I kept asking Divine to help me survive. The answer was always: **"You will not only survive. You will thrive."**

It was several years before I would describe myself as thriving. A lot of counseling and soul searching accompanied my meditation and spiritual growth.

During this time my grandfather and my dad chose to disown me. They both went to legal lengths to formally disavow me as their relation because of my memories of being molested. This was a devastating time, as well as a very sad and lonely time which divided my family.

Eventually I did thrive and, much to my surprise, I even went on to love and marry again seven years later.

Divine took a firm hold of guiding me to people, sources, and books. Books literally fell right off the bookstore shelves, falling at my feet.

There were some disquieting and discomforting things going on in my body now. My arms were numb and hurting. I had muscles twitching on their own without my control. I was scheduled to have a nerve conduction test in Denver about three hours drive away, in very snowy conditions, which would make it necessary for me to wake up at 4:00 a.m. I would also have to rouse two sleeping children at that early hour. I lay in bed and tried to convince myself that my problem actually was better and certainly my condition did not warrant the long early drive with two babies in tow. I lay my head back onto the pillow to snuggle down for some additional sleep I was convinced was more necessary. Suddenly all the lights in my home flashed ON. No one else was home and yet I heard someone yell, **"I'm trying to tell you!"** Well, let me tell you, I was out of bed, showered, and on the road before I really woke up, or even thought about "what just happened!"

The reason I was seemingly shoved out of bed with such strange happenings became very clear later. The doctor found pinched nerves in my neck, shoulder, and arms. The doctor sent me for physical therapy and massage. The woman I saw for physical therapy and massage was very spiritually aware. She became my first mentor and teacher on this spiritual journey as a psychic medium.

I took a class called Awakening Your Light Body from 1992-1993. In this class my meditation was transformed and my intuition became much stronger.

In 1994 I was still single and struggling in every aspect of my life. I was working full time and caring for my children after work. After they went to bed I would do a reading for one or two people. I was exhausted and so was my bank account.

April 16, 1994 I woke up to a mantra being sung in my head. *There are no major decisions. There are no major decisions. There are no major decisions.* I had realized the previous night that I was out of money and would very quickly be out of credit. I knew if my ex-husband didn't pay $24,000.00 in back child support, something he seemed to have no intention of doing, I would be out of money with zero credit in a matter of days. I would be in big trouble! I had been living on credit because the income I made covered only rent and almost covered daycare but was not enough for food, diapers, gas, clothing, medical, or anything else! The mantra helped me to see that I needed to check in with God about this. Again the answer was, **"There are no major decisions. You have no options left."** That day I lost my job and couldn't pay daycare anymore anyway. No daycare=no job. No job=no daycare $$. Rent would take up more than I had remaining in credit. Suddenly this was not a major decision but an emergency. I needed to move to California where I could live with family and have free day care until I could get a job and get on my feet. I moved to California with the children on May 11th, 1994.

In California we moved in with my mom. I worked for Hooked on Phonics as an accountant and handled the accounting for *The Doctor Laura Show*.

Over Memorial Day weekend in 1995 *The Orange County Register* ran an article about me as a psychic expert. My phone rang off the hook. *The Tustin Daily* and *The Independent* ran articles around this time as well. I was devoted to motherhood and juggling my accounting job as well as offering my readings in the evening, after my kids went to bed at night.

One night during this period I had a dream.

I am in a mustard-color 1974 Datsun B210 with my two little cherubs in the back seat. I am in the passenger seat as we navigate through the high mountain beauty. The car comes to a curve but continues straight off the road. I expect the car will turn around. However, it continues directly off the pavement. All at once I was aware the entire road ended and it ended quite abruptly. The car hung in the air over a cliff (yes, much like a cartoon). There was a drop-off to the ground below. It was like going off a cliff (a leap of Faith). Here was this deep crevasse below the car and yet I felt a very pointed peace. I rather calmly said to myself, "We're going off now." During the time that flashed quickly past I remember thinking I should wake the kids, but then we were landed so quickly. We missed every obstacle including a card table and various home furnishings already on the ground, as well as the solid granite face of the mountain, just inches from the front bumper. We landed in what looked like a small campground. We landed so softly as if settled in a cloud. The kids woke up and bounced out of the car. They just said "woooow" and began to play and giggle. I couldn't get over the beauty of the little canyon we landed in and the gentle landing. We landed so softly, like a toy car being gently laid down by the hand of God. Life was simple here and we were happy with fewer belongings.

I knew this dream represented the leap of faith I needed to make. I also new life would be simple and happy and safe, as the dream represented.

I woke up with the words from a song in the Disney movie *Pocahontas*. The lyrics were reminding me of the wonders and riches of nature and the beauty all around us. The lyrics told me not to measure my decision to move on by material safety. I was beginning to feel more convinced about the coming changes.

The next night I woke up with lyrics to a song in my head assuring me that I would find gold and jewels, indicating I would be financially safe. I was really getting a strong guidance to quit my job, move on, and that we would be okay financially.

The following night yet another song woke me up. This time a little jingle within a song from the movie *Lion King*, which advised me to listen to teacher and be prepared for sensational news.

Clearly my children and I had watched these movies and the songs were not unknown to me. Spirit has often used a repeated lyric, from a song stuck in my head that I could not ignore, as a way to give me a message. Often the jingle immediately has a very clear meaning to me. The three nights in a row of singing messages were soothing, like a warm oil of reassurance that everything would be fine financially as I quit our main source of income and security.

I took the "Leap of Faith" and I quit my accounting job which included health insurance, sick leave, holidays, and most of all a secure paycheck! My first week's income as an intuitive channel matched what I had been making as an accountant!! Wow, that was a miracle.

At this time I was invited to join The Orange County Society for Psychic Research, OCSPR. I was a speaker and teacher for several meetings of OCSPR and met several people with gifts similar to mine. I was asked to investigate various haunted places in and around Orange County. I had many adventures in ghost busting with this amazing group.

In 1996 I was asked by a friend to come and look at a home she was purchasing. While walking through the home, I stopped at the handrail overlooking the living area. I was overcome with emotions—good ones—very moving emotions and I told her. *"Someone is going to get married here or because of this home."*

About a year later I was invited to this home to celebrate her birthday with her and friends. I did not know anyone at the party except for her and her husband. I was having fun meeting everyone. At one point I was standing in the family room with about five or six men just chatting, maybe flirting just a little. Someone asked me the traditional question of what do you do? Imagine this scene because it's really quite funny.

I said, "I am a professional Psychic."

Fast as lightning it seemed that the room emptied out. Five men were saying how cool that was for an occupation as they were backing away as fast as they could. It seemed as if they were afraid I could read something about them. I was used to this; it happened with most men.

Almost immediately, there was only one man left in the room. He was very handsome and stood in front of me with his hand extended. He said, "How cool is that! I have been reading a book about intuition, can you read my palm?"

I don't read palms and never have, but to humor him I took his hand in mine palm side up. I traced my finger along the smooth warm skin of his palm as I made up a bunch of great "stuff." Only I wasn't making it up, I was receiving the information from Spirit while I held his palm in mine.

We hung out with each other the remainder of the night playing pool and dancing. That was November 15, 1997 and we have never been apart since that night.

Apparently, it was I who was the one to get married because of the house. My bridal shower was held in that home as well.

I invite you now to join me on an adventure of Spirit and to explore many of the messages that have been shared through me over time. I hope you will enjoy the wisdom and peace that Spirit offers and perhaps see yourself in some of the situations. I find that one

THE BEGINNING

person's questions and guidance can many times speak to a place in all of us. I hope the questions and the response of Divine knowledge satisfy some of your deep yearnings inside of you. It is my hope that the answers here will satisfy some of your own questions and offer you some comfort. May the light of Divine Love always shine a light on your personal journey.

KNOWING

ONE

FINDING YOUR INTUITIVE VOICE

I have been helping people obtain clarity, achieve peace, and secure hope for over twenty-nine years. I feel very blessed to be gifted as a psychic channel, spiritual counselor, and intuitive healer. It is deeply rewarding to help others by helping people to receive the guidance they need to attract love and financial success. It gives me great joy to help people receive the answers they need to achieve their dreams.

People come to me for a variety of reasons. Many come to me with issues of the heart and issues with family relationships. People also seek information about their career path, and information about their health. Others come because they need to make an important decision. I offer clear guidance with all these life situations. No question is too small or insignificant. I find that any question is worthy.

Some people come to me seeking spiritual counseling as an alternative to traditional psychotherapy. I help people create change that they are excited to embrace.

Important decisions can be overwhelming and paralyzing at the same time. I chose to write this book to inform and help you identify and hear your personal intuitive voice. It will help you find the information you need for personal guidance.

We all have intuition. It is natural to all of us, and we all use our intuition all the time. However, we aren't always aware that some of our decisions and choices are made with intuition. Much like a muscle, it can be exercised and strengthened. If you are interested in strengthening your intuition as well as learning to trust your intuition, you will need to practice. Any skill you wish to develop takes practice. Being gifted certainly helps. Just as some people find musical instruments easy and another person may pick up math concepts with no problem, we all have areas of strength that are more natural to our character.

A mother may not know why she knows her child is in danger. She just knows, and with certainty! We call this Mother's Intuition. Intuition is perceiving directly from the Source. Intuition is an experience of knowing, without assistance from people or things such as tarot cards, pictures, etc.

Intuition is something all people experience and use all the time whether they are aware of it or not. We all get ideas, creative inspiration, or a feeling of fear without apparent cause. Perhaps you have known who was calling you before you picked up the phone.

Often our intuition speaks to us in the same voice as our mind chatter. It is a very familiar voice, which "feels" and "sounds" within the mind, just like our own thoughts. This is because it is our own thoughts, and this is why the practice is needed, to help us discern between our two inner voices. With a lot of practice it is possible to distinguish which thoughts or feelings have an origin in the conscious mind and which originate from a sixth sense or guidance from Divine Spirit. Our intuition connects us to a more subtle frequency of communication and, when we are not experienced, it can be very difficult to decipher the difference.

Intuition grows more and more clear the more it is recognized and followed. It is important to trust and even acknowledge in some way that you have just received intuitive information. Just writing down or recording these insights is a way of honoring them as being of value to you. Acknowledge your gratitude that you have been offered this insight, perhaps by saying thank you. You can also create the feeling of thankfulness even without uttering a word.

My mother gave me good advice when I was young. She told me first of all that intuition was nothing to be afraid of. Secondly she always told me to think of intuition as any other skill or muscle—the more you use it, practice, honor it and nurture it, the bigger and stronger it will grow!

I believe it is very important to understand at least a little bit about the beliefs of any guide you will be consulting. All information coming through another person will have some of their vibration or beliefs attached. A person that is consumed with end of times and dark energy will bring that through in your reading. Just the same someone with a very spiritual and loving base will be more likely to read for you with a positivity to the reading. It is important to understand the style of the reader as well as where they get their information.

The word "Psychic" is often used as a catch all term for any form of knowing the unseen realm. Psychic work is anything that involves sensitivity to non-physical or supernatural nature. The normal means by which we gather and process information relies on our five senses of sight, taste, hearing, touch, smell. Psychic work is the process of obtaining information without using these methods. In psychic work, extra-sensory (beyond the senses) methods are used to gain insight into people, events or situations that would otherwise not be available to the normal range of senses. An example of this would be reading

FINDING YOUR INTUITIVE VOICE

the personality of someone over the phone, whom you have not yet met. When talking about intuition and psychic ability many people use the two terms interchangeably.

Psychic—Originates from the Greek word *psychikos* 1855-60 and simply means of the soul or non-physical.

People who are gifted with intuition may receive their information in different ways. Some intuitives hear information, while others visually see a sign or vision inside of themselves.

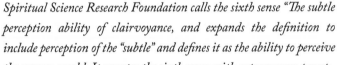

Spiritual Science Research Foundation calls the sixth sense "The subtle perception ability of clairvoyance, and expands the definition to include perception of the "subtle" and defines it as the ability to perceive the unseen world. It equates the sixth sense with extrasensory perception (ESP), premonition and dimension" or unseen realm of angels, ghosts and heaven.

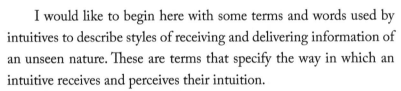

I would like to begin here with some terms and words used by intuitives to describe styles of receiving and delivering information of an unseen nature. These are terms that specify the way in which an intuitive receives and perceives their intuition.

Clairvoyant—The power to perceive things that are not physically present. Intuition in the form of seeing visions or pictures. An example of clairvoyance is seeing the aura around a living thing, or seeing an event before it takes place. I have this ability. Sometimes I am so immersed in a vision while I am having it, that I have a 365-degree knowledge of what is happening. Oftentimes I can hear what is going on and even feel the feelings of those involved.

Clairaudient—This refers to intuition that is heard in an audible way. Some of the greatest composers have said they hear the music and then they write it down.

I am often told verbally exactly what to say to my client. At times I only know the simple answer to the question is a yes or a no or perhaps a specific name. When I am receiving intuitive information in a clairaudient way it may not be important for me to understand the answer for myself at all. Only to respect it and repeat it accurately is most important. Sometimes Divine Spirit will protect another person's privacy in this way. At these times it is only important that they receive the answer. To have me understand every detail is perhaps distracting or more intimate knowledge than they wish me to be aware of. In this way I only know the simple answer to the question being asked.

Sixth sense of smell—as far as I know there is not a word such as clairolfactory. This is Intuition that is smelled. For example the aura of a person has a smell. I have the sixth sense of smell and I can tell you that it is sometimes a blessing and sometimes a curse. This is where the slang comment may come from, "this stinks."

Sixth sense of taste—Intuition in the form of taste is seldom used as a tool for doing a reading, but is very handy in the kitchen.

Clairsentient and Empathic are frequently used as interchangeable terms. This refers to someone who has empathy or sympathy. Even more than this it refers to the gift of a deep knowing of the other person's experience as well as the emotional and physical feeling associated with the experience. If you empathize with your child you may feel sad for them when they are feeling sad. A true Clairsentient, however, can feel the feelings or illness in themselves, just the same as the person they are helping is feeling. I have this ability. When my child would scrape a knee for example, I would actually feel the pain in my own knee.

This is a very potent trait in a Healer. It can also cause some very serious problems for a Clairsentient. I have on occasion become sick to my stomach or felt pain in some other place in my body or felt strong emotions suddenly. At those times I have come to recognize it is coming from a client that is about to show up at my door. I have become very good at adjusting my perceptions at these times so that I can feel what is troubling them, but feel it "within them" where it originates. This of course becomes very important to a Clairsentient. In my classes on healing, I teach Clairsentients how to feel other people's feelings or symptoms while leaving them in the other person. It is vitally important for a true Healer to learn to feel the symptoms where they originate. Repeatedly taking on the symptoms of the person we are helping can make us ill and emotionally unstable or at the least quite unclear. As an intuitive it is critical to know where you end and where the other person begins.

Empathy means "beside symptoms." This means you are fully aware of the depth and intensity of any particular emotion, thought, or situation, but are not personally affected by it. For example, we may have a friend who is experiencing grief—we are able to literally feel and experience the depth of their sadness, but we still keep one foot in our own space so that we do not identify with it or make it our own.

Clairsentience is a strong healing force because it allows people to share in a deep and spiritual way what they are experiencing for another person. Sometimes we feel like people around us don't really "get" how bad it is, but a Clairsentient actually does. A proper Clairsentient healer will simultaneously perceive where and how you are, while maintaining their own perspective. This allows me to be "in" your experience and objective at the same time. In this way I am able to help you get to a new paradigm of healing, in a quick and effective way. Motivated Clairsentients and empaths can learn how to control their empathic abilities, to create personal, energetic, and spiritual boundaries.

We have talked about ways in which an intuitive person is gifted in receiving knowledge. Now I would like to share with you different sources from which they might receive their intuitive messages.

When seeking psychic or intuitive guidance it becomes important to understand where your consultant receives their information. I consider this to come mostly from two categories, one being the use of tools, such as cards and palm reading. The other source, which is considered to be more advanced and pure, is called intuitive channeling or psychic mediumship. I am gifted in intuitive channeling and psychic mediumship.

Palm readings and tarot readings are examples of intuitive tools a reader might use to call forth information. The reader is reading information from their tools, which are then interpreted. These tools have guidelines that can be learned and memorized. They have long-standing accuracy in their tradition but still must be interpreted. The best interpretation will occur when the reader has years of experience and is gifted with intuition as well. Then through their experience and knowledge of the tools, interpretation is necessary before conveying it across to the client or seeker.

Tarot card readers, palm and face readers, as well any other reading that involves the use of tools, requires knowledge of the art. Once the symbolic meaning is known, the reader will gather the knowledge told in the cards or other tools. In order to convey the message to the seeker, they must first process the images, words, feelings, sounds, etc. through their own intuition. They must then relay the information in a way that makes sense to the person they are guiding. Therefore, these types of tools and work involve a lot more interpretation from the person reading for you. This will leave you, the client, in a position of more vulnerability to the personality of the reader. Someone else is interpreting guidance meant for you.

FINDING YOUR INTUITIVE VOICE

The exception to this is in the case of a **psychic channel or medium** who is actually allowing Spirit to speak through them. This would be considered the second way that an intuitive might gather information for you. I prefer these methods because they are the most pure. No reading of tools or interpretation is involved during a channeled session.

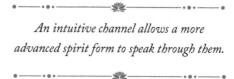

An intuitive channel allows a more advanced spirit form to speak through them.

Channel and Medium are often used interchangeably to describe a gifted and evolved intuitive who is able to temporarily set aside their own self in the interest of allowing a much more advanced presence to speak through them in service to others. A channel is able to tune out their rational mind, ego, logical and personal belief system to allow messages to flow through them. Channel work can be very difficult for most humans because everyone has very strong personal beliefs and ideals of their own. In channeling one must become indifferent to the wisdom coming through them. The Channel must not evaluate or judge the information in any way. Any concern about the message, or the way it is being delivered, is an interruption associated with ego and has no place in a channeled session. During the process of channeling, the Channel is bringing through the entire personality of the Spirit and must set aside their own person, as I do in a trance state. If at any time the Channel becomes concerned about the information and lets their own ego become involved, purity of the information can be lost.

One of the very earliest channeled readings I gave was affected because my own thinking got involved. The woman who had come to see me was very old. We had already discussed some health issues

FINDING YOUR INTUITIVE VOICE

as well as the fact that she had a prosthetic leg. I heard (clairaudient) "You will die swiftly!" I immediately thought, *oh no, there is no way I am saying that to her.* Again I heard "You will die swiftly." I was in my conscious mind again as I thought, *This can't be good. I absolutely cannot tell this sweet little old lady such upsetting news!* The voice came again saying, "Tell her she will die swiftly, not soon...swiftly!" I spoke the words to her as instructed. She began weeping and crying with relief. She was overjoyed with this news and explained that this was the entire reason for her trip to see a psychic. All of her friends were dying slow and painful deaths from cancer and she was scared. She was seeking, more than any other news, confirmation that her death would be swift.

An intuitive channel allows a more advanced spiritual form to speak through them. That is the beauty of this type of sacred gift and must be honored with complete surrender and without human ego. In most cases the channeled messages are coming through from a source that is very familiar, known and trusted by the Channel. The source I channel is the same source I have considered God to be and have prayed to all my life. You will hear me refer to this source as God, Divine, or Spirit.

My work, my being, and the entire reason for my existence is to cele-brate our Creator, whom I refer to as Divine, God, or Holy Spirit. I use several words to mean God. In every case I am referring to a single source of creation in the universe. I don't ever intend to impress my religious or spiritual views on anyone. I hope you will insert whatever name suits you best in describing the Omnipresent energy of the Creator.

You will notice that the personality, voice, and gestures are usually very different while the intuitive is Trance Channeling. That is, they express as a different person entirely from their own life expression. Think of intuitive channeling as a message coming to you through me as if I am a telephone line. Words coming through unchanged and in the voice of the person on the other end of the telephone wire. In this case Spirit is on the other end of the line. This is what was meant when Spirit spoke to me saying, "Telegraphing. We can speak through you if you will allow it." The indication that I would be as a telephone wire between Spirit and an earthbound soul seeking some form of guidance.

Even after I agreed to be of service in this way, that was just the beginning of my learning. There was a great deal of training, discipline, and practice that followed before I was able to Trance Channel with purity.

Medium is another description used for a Channel; however, it may also be used to describe a person gifted in reaching loved ones that have passed over. In some cases you will find Mediums that can talk to your loved ones and friends on the other side. Most commonly they will tell you about them, and convey messages but not allow the person themselves to emerge through them. I offer mediumship in this way. It is very dangerous and exhausting to actually let any variety of soul come through you as you speak. This is not a quality judgment of anyone's loved ones or relatives. Regardless of how evolved the loved one may have been, it is too much changing of frequencies for the medium.

Mediumship of loved ones can offer such a valuable gift for those grieving. Mediumship is also valuable to earthbound loved ones wishing to resolve issues or questions left unresolved at the time of another person's passing.

I am a Psychic Medium and sometimes people ask about loved ones on the other side. I am sharing a reading next that involves a person that felt that someone was trying to communicate with her from the "other side." She felt a little skeptical and silly thinking that. She came to me and asked if I could check in with Spirit, and ask if anyone was trying to communicate with her. In the reading, two pieces of advice are given to help with developing intuition, 1) to set aside time to meditate and 2) write down information that you hear or think you hear coming to you.

When I allow Holy Spirit to speak through me I literally step aside and become an open flute for Spirit's words. I become an observer, much like the experience you might have while observing yourself during a dream. Because I allow myself to be used as a voice by Spirit, my demeanor changes. You may also notice that the accent, cantor and timber of my voice changes. The very energy of the room transforms.

Throughout this book I share exerts of readings from clients. Because I am not directly reading the words but allowing them to manifest through me, you may notice the use of language and grammar can be somewhat unique. I have purposely not edited the voice of Spirit. I put the voice of Spirit in italics, and questions from seekers in quotations.

Sheila's Reading:

You are mostly connected to Spirit, and sort of know and sort of don't know this. You understand? You kind of get it and kind of don't. You are the only obstacle between you and the consciousness. You feel it sometimes good and sometimes not at all.

"I feel like someone wants to connect with me and I just don't know how."

What we are saying is similar. There is just the thinnest veil between you and them. There really is communication now and you question it. You question 'Do I really get this or is it like this for all people?'

The sense of not quite being able to trust it exists because it is not an audible hearing for you. It is a heart hearing for you. The angel wings are right there, so you can almost hear them flapping. But you feel and know, more than hear. You sense and know, but do not trust.

*A being joins us now. If we are looking at it with human eyes, it is androgynous. Often when talking to angel beings it is as such. For this one trying to talk to you, it is male. What he says is "I want you to get it!" He is not really having a temper tantrum, but is most frustrated with you. Good humoredly, but he is frustrated. He wants you to get it; he is saying..."*It is not a one-time deal. I want a dialog. I want communication, a dialog. It is not for you to go and get information. It is for US to talk." *He is agitated and frustrated.*

"Frustrated with my lack of ability?"

No. What he is saying is, "It is like we are trying to dance together and you are stepping on my feet, and I am stepping on your feet." *He knows that you SOMETIMES know what he has said or what he has meant. He gets frustrated that you don't trust what you know you have heard. What his suggestion is, and we agree with it, would be to go into a prayerful or meditative stillness not trying to hear him. But developing your ability to just be quiet. As you would in prayer, you feel something, you feel a difference of opening. So we do agree with this. He is suggesting that you say your prayer and then you be quiet and just be there for five to ten minutes. Not straining to listen but more to say,* "Open me that I might know." *And he says it is not all you. It is us learning together. He is trying to communicate also. Wants to do this together.*

Get a notebook. Then when you do know or you think you know information, write it down. He is a lot more interested in this as an adventure together. Interested in an ongoing dialog.

"So, he is not trying to convey one particular message to me?"

He says, "A word or two could not convey my intention or my feelings. It would be like going to a craft store and buying a poster someone else made. Instead of creating one yourself." *He says,* "We will have none of that!"

He says, "I want to paint together, I want to play together, like this. Okay?" *He is very serious. He is not a cuckoo, nor a frivolous kind of guy.*

"No. If it is who I think it is, he is not."

He is taking this very seriously. A game he wants to play with you together. Learning the skill.

You are very close. You just tend to be a perfectionist. You don't want to write it down unless you are absolutely sure. He is saying, "Loosen up a little." *Even if you just think you might have heard something. Write it down. He is wanting to teach you to be a medium or channel of your own type. It doesn't mean you change careers. But he says you never know. It can be an option.*

"I want to know who this is because I have a feeling I know who he is. Did I know him?"

Oh yes. (He giggles.) He says, "Of course you did. Brother."
It feels very brotherly. Brother of yours?

"I have two brothers, but they are both alive."

The closeness of best friends, but brotherly.
He is saying that you are very closely related. It is Jim.

"Oh, my brother-in-law!"

He is doing a silly dance to say, "Yeah, you got it right!"

I have chosen to share this next reading because it was given as a lesson to help Jewel to develop further on her spiritual journey. It is a teaching that will help you to recognize and develop your intuition.

A Reading for Jewel:

Greetings! We are very pleased to be with you. You have a very lot of intuitive and occult understanding in your past that you brought with you as talents in this life. Deep comprehension of things occult. Occult not meaning anything more than what it means, "unseen world." You have what we would call a lot of knowledge in the unseen world. It has been a part of you in many incarnations. We see here written many different aspects of your soul nature. You have been a Gypsy with experience in herbal and potion medicine. Much broad knowledge that you bring with you from many incarnations. Because of this, you are very intuitive just because there is so much knowledge in your own self. You have a tendency to have visions, and understanding of them when you do. Still working on accepting them it seems. Trying to sift reality from the vision. We would say it is mostly intuition, when you are trying to sift through it and determine if it is intuition or reality. For now just assume it is intuition. The physical is the unreal. What we recommend, dear one, is more writing down of the thoughts and less interpreting of the thoughts. There are dreams and visions. Your style comes to you in a variety. Because information comes from so many different places, it is better if you don't interpret, just know.

Trust all as real for now, and take at face value. It is not for evaluating. For you it is in honoring. Say, "I received this and I value receiving communication so I will value it enough to write it down."

You tend to get a dream or vision and you think you might have a knowing about it, but you can't figure out what the meaning is. You are at this early stage, and you are getting a lot of mixed forms of information. Just as a message on Instagram looks different than on Facebook, and the message could be the same or different in meaning. For now only record exactly what you see. Exactly as the message or vision is given. Record all of it. You are getting caught up and derailed with the interpretation of it all. You are not at the place to interpret. You are getting information you can receive, but you are not able to understand yet. For now do not be worried if it is wrong. In time you will gain the ability to discern the meaning of it all. First and foremost when you get something or think maybe you sort of did, write it down. Do include a date. Please, when you feel something, or know it, if you will pause and take a moment. Ask—is there more? You want to stay as neutral as possible. When you begin to interpret, you are in the earthly mind. You are starting to get information and then you arrest it by thinking. You are kicked out of that intuitive place when you are into the human thinking mind. Interpretation can come later.

We recommend for you a few tools. Try to find what you would call a symbol dictionary or today you may be able to find an internet site for symbols. When you see a symbol, draw it, just record the vision. Flip through pages to see what you saw in your vision. When you look it up, then write down exactly what it says for the symbol. Then try to figure out what does it mean to me. Three stages to this. Sometimes you will know when it is a spirit animal or something to be looked up from that aspect.

Right now you are at a stage when you are getting just one symbol or one word. So let's look at "bunny" for example and give you an idea. A bunny could mean a few different things. You may know someone known by the name of Bunny. You may be wondering if someone you know is honest and transparent or manipulative as in magic. Like pulling a bunny from a hat. If you have been asking it so, the bunny may indicate to you a bit of deception as in magic. There are also meanings associated with bunny as a symbol of multiplying as bunnies do create very quickly. This can be a sign of abundance regarding what you are asking about. Bunny as totem animal or bunny as personality trait. So the bunny is a simple form of intuition or communication to you. First acknowledge bunny has been received as a message. As with the symbols, you would be wise to look up all of the information and associated meanings for bunny and record these without yet any interpretation.

Separately you can begin to examine what you have collected. You may find that a meaning begins to emerge. We find that at this stage you are at with one symbol or word intuition, the word or picture will often be repetitive in the same vision or several versions of bunny in this case. See?

Dreams for some can be so very informative. We do advise that you record your dreams. For this to work properly you must record the dream just as you awaken. We find that it will work best if you do not, as much as possible, move when you awaken. Have your note pad and pencil close at hand so you can stay almost asleep as you recite the dream onto the paper. As we said to you before, the interpretation must be at an entirely different time or you will begin to alter the dream as you get into the human interpretive mind.

If you are interested in getting a dream journal for yourself, it is preferable to go to a bookstore where you can look through several dream books. You can't pick the wrong one, because there is no wrong one. They are all written with knowledge and wise intent. It is to pick the one that most feels right to you. You must pick only one for this to work. If you pick more than one you will be second-guessing all of your dreams. Bring the book home and thumb through it. Even better if you can quickly read through all of it, but without trying at all to remember. Your subconscious will take care of that for you. You may sleep with it under your pillow or travel through it in your mind's eye during meditation. You will then say to your higher self: Look this is the book I will use to interpret my dreams so let's agree to use this as the tool. Whatever a peach means here in this book, is what a peach will mean in my dreams. Now you have added a tool to your interpretation.

I really encourage you to make meditation a regular and devoted part of daily life if you wish to increase and clarify your personal intuition. Meditation is the number one advice I hear from Spirit for those who wish to increase their intuition. Intuition is a gift that naturally awakens as you become adept at tuning in to what I call Divine. You won't be able to hear the intuitive guidance of Spirit if you are not able to tune out the external five senses. Devoted time to meditation will help your intuitive development more than any other thing you can do.

Enjoy exploring and opening to your personal intuitive voice. It is very helpful to keep a journal of experiences which can validate your intuitive insights, and also teach you about mistaking mind chatter for intuition.

TWO

ROMANTIC RELATIONSHIPS

Right home, right husband, right now!" There was that booming voice in my head.

I have a nightly ritual of prayer and meditation. I don't ask for intuitive guidance during this time, but sometimes it comes through anyway.

"Right home, Right husband, Right now!"

As a single mother working a full-time accounting job and also offering intuitive readings, I had no time and little interest in dating. I could count the first dates I had accepted on just one hand. No second dates needed, thank you very much! My life was happy and plenty full. After my divorce I was still very much wondering if marital bliss was a reality or a myth.

I have learned to always follow the guidance I receive, so three days later on Saturday I looked for a new place to live. I found a great new home and signed a lease. The following Saturday I went to a friend's birthday party and met my husband. In less than two weeks my life had changed. I am glad, to say the least, that I did follow my intuitive guidance. I want to help you understand your personal, intuitive guidance so you can create a better love life too.

Relationship is by far one of the topics that most people include in their questions at a reading. Even if it is not the core reason to seek intuitive guidance, it seems to find its way into each and every consultation. This is because we are all in relationships of one sort or another from the moment of birth, and relating can get complicated. It all starts with your relationship with Yourself, and I imagine you may have heard this before. Then bring in parents and perhaps siblings, who greatly affect our perceptions of love and relationships. They are our first and most powerful teachers when we are young and most absorbent of our life paradigms.

This chapter is going to be focused around romantic types of love. As you will begin to notice, though, we never get away from some of our core beliefs and they tend to continue their permeation of all our other varied relationships.

Please, if possible, set aside your perception of male and female gender differences here. We all have aspects of both male and female energy or personality traits within us. When I refer to male and female energy here I am referring to the dominating energy being expressed by the soul and not the specific physical gender that we see. In both heterosexual and homosexual relationships there is a balance of male and female energy being expressed by each person as well as the relationship itself. I will be referring to dominant energy and the balance of male vs. female energy. When I refer to male energy, I am talking about energy which initiates, or exerts, gives, extends and seeks. Female energy referred to here is that energy which is receptive in nature, meaning it receives and reflects. Female energy is intuitive, creative. Neither initiating or receptive energy is better or lesser than the other. However, one may serve you better than another in creating the kind of balanced relationship you dream of.

Male energy is that energy that provides. Goes out, hunts down the bear or the bacon, and brings it home to the feet of the female energy. The male energy craves conquest and challenges that require external thrust. The first clue in which we see this is the sexual act and even the given equipment on the male body. The male energy gives, dominates, decides, extends. Thinking of the male energy as the sun helps me.

Now, all you girls out there that are bringing home the bacon too (thank you very much!) don't get your panties in a bunch over these definitions. No one is all male or all female energy and to some extent it is a choice. Just follow me for a bit. This all balances out when we get to the good stuff—Love.

Female energy is the receiver, passive, emotional, and the reflector. Softer bodies, receiving bodies, less muscular by design. Again a clue can be taken from the bodies of women. The female energy is likened to the moon. The moon takes in the sun and reflects it back to light the night. The light is softer and yet just as important and relevant in its own way. This is not a new concept. The idea of Yin and Yang has been around for thousands of years. Yang is male energy and yin is female energy and we aim for a balance in all things. Female's bodies are made to gather, create, nest, nurture, reproduce, but of course that is not all they are capable of.

Women now make up a large percentage of the workforce. In order to excel in the area of career, women have needed to develop a more masculine energy. This has been necessary to compete in a male designed, left brain work environment. But is it causing relationship confusion, havoc and loneliness? I certainly see a direct correlation here.

ROMANTIC RELATIONSHIPS

I have owned my own business for twenty-nine years. I have been a single mother of two children and didn't receive child support for several of those years. It is certainly impossible to be **only** the feminine receiving energy, when there is not a male energy providing! Out of need many of the women on the planet have changed their dominant energy to be more male dominant in order to survive. Men have changed as well but to a lesser degree. Male energy still wins in commerce and the male role at work has not changed much. The goals in the workplace are the same and they harmonize well with male energy. Go win, conquer, get to the top.

As our culture has evolved to one where many women work outside of the home, men have needed to adapt to changes as well. Men are adjusting to female bosses and coworkers. At home men have been asked to pitch in and help with house care, as well as care-giving of children. No more of the stereotype of pipe and slippers meeting them at the door. This service with a smile in the fifties might have been delivered by a housewife with a home all neatly put together. Today she may be getting home later than he is from work. Men are preparing dinners and tending to children as well as their spouses. They are sharing feelings more than they used to. Most men still prefer to be acknowledged for what they accomplished and how intelligently they do it. We all like to be respected, and it is a reflection of male energy to desire respect.

I bring this subject of male and female energy up because I have seen relationships transform overnight when couples get in touch with what they really want in relationships and how this translates to male or female dominance in themselves and their partners. Once they have been able to adopt the practice of letting male or female energy domi-nate in their relationships, a harmonious balance is created for all. Not all women want to be taken care of and not all men want to take down and drag home the bear. So find the type of balance that is natural for you and your needs and the expectations of your partner.

This is a good chance to think of same sex couples. Let go of any expectations of who should be responsible for doing or not doing anything. In a relationship such as this would you rather be leading and valued for your thoughts? On the other hand, would you rather create and feel, and with this be cherished for your feeling and nurturing nature?

When it comes to attracting a partner it is crucial to get in touch with your thoughts and feelings on this matter. Most people find they are not all one or the other, but a balance. The point is to decide what is most important to you. With this the key is to also become very clear on what you do or do not want in a partner.

I work with plenty of women who are very strong, capable, and successful. Some are also very much alone and lonely even though they are attractive, bright, and amazing women. I have many male clients who are lonely too, and they tell me about women who have emasculated them and made them feel useless, small, and not valued.

To the women who prefer a strong male type and want to be the feminine energy in the relationship I hear Divine guidance quite often say, *"Don't bring your work self home with you."* By this Spirit is talking to the powerful male dominant women among you that are in charge and amazing at your job, but want to come home and be the female energy in your relationship. You may be male dominant at work and if you are the boss or a business owner, there is not a question that it is necessary, but you can choose to leave it at the office. After all, if you are working all day in a navy blue suit that says you are all business, it would not be unusual to change into something softer and sexier. Perhaps you allow the softer and more sensual part of your personality to come out in your dating as well.

ROMANTIC RELATIONSHIPS

Barb asks:

"I have had three marriages to feminine men and I have been miserable. I love the book you recommended, but I am still confused. I have a lot of male energy, so does this mean I need to look for a feminine man?"

A feminine male would be easy for you to attract, but what you have realized is that feminine men do not make you happy. You have found great success in business through your personal male energy.

When we are talking about romance, however, you may choose to soften your male energy and increase the feminine energy within you in general, especially around men and dating. You will be happier with a male dominant man. A male dominant man has no need of fulfillment from a male dominant female. You just haven't been getting what you want in relationships. So if you change what you put forward as well as what you are looking for you will find more relationship balance and satisfaction.

There is a control issue here as well. You are afraid to let go of the reins and allow a male energy to lead. This is quite all right if you prefer to attract a softer male to follow your lead, but you are telling us you do not prefer that.

Think of this as dancing. One person needs to lead and one person needs to follow. If it doesn't go this way and both are trying to lead there will be much stepping of feet as well as chaos on the dance floor. It is not our concern whether you are the initiator (leading) or the receiver (following) energy in your relationship. Simply you will want a balance of leading and following, or everyone ends up with a failed dance, bruises, and trying to get back up off of the floor.

Enough about this male-female thing. Let's move on to what I call "The moth to the flame." The moth does not actually know why it flies right into the fire any more than most of us are aware of what it is about that certain someone across the room that has caught our attention. Sure, it is often something about that first impression. The thing is, that first impression is more than looks. There is a vibration emanating from that person and you are picking up what they are putting down. In the universe everything has an energy field, and this is what I am referring to here as vibration. You are always broadcasting who you are and so is everyone else.

Have you found that you have a repeated pattern to the partners you are choosing? Even though you may have sworn off of User and Taker personality types, you find yourself attracted to that Hot person in the room, and you don't notice all the caution bells going off. Sometimes to break out of this, Divine Spirit will recommend to date several men or women that you would not usually consider to be your type. If your type has always been the "not so good for you" type, let's see you try out some types that you really don't know all that well. The Over Giver, might be fun for a change, but you would have to be willing to receive. If you have never attracted this one, perhaps you don't know how to receive.

Olivia from Michigan had a reading over the phone and asked this question:

> "Why does every guy I date always expect me to do everything? They never want to splurge on me or take me anywhere special. I come up with all the ideas and I keep paying. I wait on them and give so much to the relationship. I really want a guy that will be there for me when I am tired

or sick. Someone who wants to be a helpmate in life. Is that too much to ask?"

Dear one, you expect to pay. You are in control from the beginning with directing the dates and planning fun activities, initiating. You must relax some and let the other party have the male energy. You are reaching to pay too fast. The male energy wants to feel the giving and providing energy. Then wants to feel smart and appreciated for his/her leadership. You are not very good at receiving. In fact you are feeling more in control when you are the giver. You are afraid to receive. Afraid you will not like what you get, for one thing. You have said that you want men with plenty of male energy. You are attracting male energy now, but you do not want to receive for fear you will have to give up control. Practice in small ways. To ask if please he would fetch a water for you, rather than to jump up and offer to get the drinks. It is true you are offering a kindness to bring water, but try to think that this one needs this opportunity to serve and you need this opportunity to receive. When you are given a gift or kindness, just say thank you.

A Giver really has no use for another Giver unless they are capable of also receiving. They get the reward they are seeking in the giving and feeling good as the giver. If you are no good at the receiving, what good are you to a Giver? They will not even feel an attraction. Users will be attracted to your over giving nature. You are attached to the control of being in your male energy. If you would rather attract male energy you must embrace more of your feminine receiving energy.

"I make good money and I don't mind paying sometimes, but I want to be taken care of the way that I want.

I really like nice things and places. I don't mind suggesting and then paying sometimes."

This is true and this can come later. However, for now you are needing to learn receiving. You are not allowing a chance for the other party to feel in charge. You very much want to have the female role and yet you will not allow yourself to receive. You have never felt cherished and cared for and this is a deep longing.

Sometimes you don't know what you want in a date if you have never known anyone of this nature. You may not even realize it exists. You have to experience that kind of relationship to learn that it exists and if it is right for you.

"Yes, but I think I don't really feel worthy. I am afraid he will not feel like I am worthy of spending dinner money on or whatever. I don't know what my role is and I just offer to pay in case my date doesn't want to."

The male that does not want to pay is usually not male energy dominant but female dominant and seeking to be taken care of.

The one who initiates the date is the male energy and they will pay for the event. Leave your pocketbook at home until you can trust yourself not to reach for your wallet and pay the bill.

The moth moves to the light because it gets confused by the light. Does it really matter to you why that guy or girl moves toward you or just that it happens?! Well, like it or not, there is an attraction to another that can be as basic to nature as the moth to the flame. For example, the ancient brain in all of us is attracted to survival. To survive we must have food and shelter and for the species to survive we must pro-create. Did you already figure out the male energy dominants are the doers and have a lot of responsibility here? They need to drag home that bear and fell a few trees to get the shelter up. Now I don't personally care who does this job, but the old brain still assigns it to men or male energy. So be it. Now men also need to pursue, capture, initiate, and insert their intentions on females or procreation doesn't take place. Guys can't help the fact that their old brain wants young and fertile women so they are more likely to reproduce and the species goes on. Nature takes care of this and men are attracted to the females that are most likely to reproduce. Those are the young ones. To the old brain this is just survival of the fittest. So, girls, those are facts. You can like them or not, but if you don't play by the rules (of old brain survival and genetics), don't whine to me.

Men and women don't always have to know what attracts them, because it's right there with the moth to the flame stuff. Women are attracted to youth and beauty as well, but it's a little bit different for women. They are also attracted to signs of strength and the ability to provide for a family. This can be especially true of female dominant women or any women who are desiring children. When it comes to survival, on some ancient level female energy knows they need a provider or they won't be able to raise the kids to adulthood. Men often complain that women just look for money and status in a man. This may not be entirely true, but a healthy young mate with years of earning power looks pretty good to the old brain. Remember the old brain in women is choosing the male that can best provide for the family during a long cold winter in the cave.

Here is what I know to be true. The law of attraction is just as real as gravity. You don't have to believe it for it to be true. Whether you believe in gravity or not, if you let go of an apple directly over your foot, an apple is going to hit your foot. If you say you just want to get married, you can and will attract just that. If you are interested in a happy healthy relationship you can have that too. You need to know what you want in order to attract it. You can forget about the law of attraction, but it is still at work giving you what you ask for, according to your habitual thinking and speaking. If you have been vague about what you want and are saying that you 'just' want someone to marry you, you are still using the law of attraction and will get vague results. Divine Spirit recommends that everyone looking for a mate, or just friendship, get clear on what they want. I will explain the best means for doing this.

If it is only in your head that you are thinking about what you are looking for in a mate, that is a great start. It does not count as setting a goal or really having intention unless you write it down. When you put an exact list together on white paper in black or blue ink, you have put something tangible into motion. Make three lists with a label at the top of each page.

The first page should say **My true love is... or My spouse is...** followed by a list of the traits he or she must have. Begin your list with the three to four most important traits in order and follow with all of the other traits this love of yours must have. While you are making this list you will probably think of some traits that you know you do not want. List these as well on another piece of paper. The heading will say anything about the traits you no longer attract. **I will no longer accept**. Don't ignore the don't wants. At the end you are going to burn this note as a sign you are done with these traits.

Now the third list and the one that is actually most important to your happiness is a list of how you want to *feel* in this relationship. Label the top of this list **When I am with my partner I feel...** The feeling list is what you really live with and experience in this relationship. Maybe you want to feel taken care of and listened to. Perhaps you want to feel respected and valued for your ideas. Do you want to feel special, respected, safe, secure, protected, nurtured, valued, or perhaps you want to feel smart, and important? You can have it all, but you must be very clear on how it is you want to feel in this relationship. Keep your list in a prominent place where you will see it often. If you like to Feng Shui your environment, the romance area is a great place for a copy of your lists as well.

At one point while I was single, Spirit had some advice for me that was very helpful. I was advised to write a quick intuitive list about a date shortly after I met them. This list was to be a quickly jotted down list of traits or whatever came to mind regarding my intuitive feeling about someone. I would write anything at all because no one but me would ever see it. I found this was very valuable if done before I ever began to develop feelings for the person.

I call this the "Good, Bad, and Ugly, Down and Dirty Truth" list. If you try this I think you will find that you are very insightful even upon a first meeting. If you see a trait in this person that is on your **I will no longer accept this list**, make a point to be very honest with yourself. If you still want to date this person, tuck the list away and don't re-read it for several dates. After a few dates read it again, and assess how accurate you were. Sometimes it is easier to be honest with yourself before you become more interested in the person. I find the more our interest grows in a potential partner, the more likely we are to embellish the good traits and disregard the questionable traits. These usually become the very traits we are frustrated or happy with after years of being a couple.

Jessica has dated George off and on for several years. When she first met him he was engaged to someone else. He told her he was leaving that relationship. Jessica later found out that George was still with his ex-fiancée for several months during the time he started dating Jessica. She has never really trusted him to be faithful. Each time they break up, it is a huge fight taking several months to simmer down. They seem to have an irresistible attraction to each other, pulling them back together again and again.

Jessica asks:

"But if he ever does get married, can he change? Will he be the same way to his wife or is it possible for him to make a commitment to one woman and stick with that?"

He can, but with you he has never been respectful of your agreement together. This is his character. It is easy to make a commitment with no real intention of holding to it whenever that commitment no longer suits him. This is the nature of him. Marriage does not change this. With intention to change he can do anything.

"If he was to decide to change, how long would that take?"

It is not measured in calendar time. It is measured in human evolutional time. How long does it take him to change? This first begins with intention and measures from there. There is no commitment yet so the measurement in calendar time is not available. At this time he does not want to change. Do you see? It is evolutionary time, not calendar date in this case.

Salli Ann is on a phone consultation with me and she is struggling to make a decision.

"What do you see for a future with me and Allan?"

He is a very nice fellow and kind to you. He is good for you. You are asking if there will be marriage? This is what you are really asking. This is not the right question because you are not free to marry. First there is another decision you need to make regarding the marriage you are in.

"Should I leave my husband then? Is that the question I should be asking? What will happen if I do that? Will I ever get married again?"

This is the question truly in the heart. You are asking if you should leave the husband, however, you only really want to know if you do leave him, will you re-marry. You are asking if you will be alone? Yes?

"Yes, I don't want to be alone. Also if I leave my husband, will I regret leaving him and how will I be financially?"

First, the correct thing that you must do is decide about the marriage based on the merits of this marriage. Not based on your fears. You have a wonderful husband, but you just do not love him. He is set in his ways and a bit dull for you, this is true. If you do not feel you can ever love this one again you rather owe to him his own freedom to find love.

"I don't think he would re-marry anyway. He only works. That is his sole interest. He never has any energy for anything else."

This is true of him in your marriage but not yours to choose for him. It will be a surprise to you that he marries rather quickly.

"But will I ever marry again?"

This is only a question if you are out of your marriage. You are trying to hedge your bets. You only wish to leave the husband if you have insurance of a new love. You must decide if you want to be married to this one, or not, based on what you have together, not based on who you may find next. He feels like an insurance policy to you. It is well known that if you make a false insurance claim you are in for big problems! It is true here as well if you stay for insurance purposes only, you will never find happiness in love. If you just want to be married...well, you are! If, however, you are telling us you would like to be in love and happily married. We can tell you that you will no longer find it in this marriage, as you are quite aware you no longer love him.

There is new love available to you....

Sue asks:

"I have been dating Trevor for four years. What is it about me that he cannot make a commitment to be exclusive?"

It is not about you. He cannot surrender to love, he cannot release. The closest he comes is when he first meets a girl. He usually thinks she is perfect and seems to fall in love immediately. As he gets to know her, reality sets in that she is a normal person and not a Goddess created in absolute perfection. He slowly cools on her but may stay interested. This he has done with you.

"Yes, when we first met he would exalt me as perfection and was just crazy about me. So if he doesn't like me anymore why does he keep asking me out?"

He cannot bring himself to make a commitment to you because he has realized you are a normal human. He will remain looking for the "perfect partner." He believes that if you just try harder or do something different/better you could be perfect and he could love you enough. Then he could commit to you. The truth is that he cannot allow himself to surrender. This also relates to his inability to ejaculate as well. He cannot commit and he cannot let go his control and melt into a relationship. He seeks perfection, which in reality does not exist.

You come from the belief system that is the perfect fit to his.

You always believe that you are not enough and that if you were just a bit better/more you could be worthy of love. He believes that he needs someone to offer more/better and then he can surrender. You believe you need to be more lovable so he will commit. He believes that he needs to find better so he can commit.

You have this attitude that if the country club would have you it must not be much of a club. So any club that would have you is not good enough for you to join. The only club worthy of joining would be one that can see how much you need to be improved upon to be worthy of joining. Any club whose standards are so low that they would let you join is not worth joining. He is a club that almost wants you but won't let you join until you improve. He is just the right club because he sees that you need to improve to be good enough.

"That sounds totally crazy, and you're right. What can I do to change this?"

This is a bit tricky because this would require you dating men who are excited to be with you. Men who adore you and find you desirable. You probably will not like them at first. We do recommend that you experience what it is like to be loved for who you are rather than your potential for improvement.

Danielle is in pharmaceutical sales and she has been asking about a new job. She is tall, statuesque, and immaculately dressed. She looks like a model. In seeing her there is an assumption that she has a very high sense of self-esteem. She has been in a relationship with Ben for five years. He asked her to marry him and move in with him almost immediately after they began dating. They have lived together unmarried for the past four and a half years. He finds a lot of faults with her and she is always trying to be more perfect so that he will finally marry her. They have just had a big fight and now he says that he does not want children. With her biological clock ticking faster every passing day, she is tired of waiting.

Danielle asks:

"What should I do, because I know he is never going to marry me now, but now is it too late for me to marry anyone else and still have children?"

It is not too late for children. You are fertile still and will be fertile until thirty-eight. You are good together, and we also see that if you do not have children you come to regret this. He has really decided and will remain mostly fixed on not having children. You must also take note that he is wanting to be selfish and even says that he likes being selfish. This you have been able to enjoy as he does spoil you as well. You would come to not like him as a father to your children. Do not stay with him because you believe you are out of time to meet another. Stay only if you are in love and can agree about children....

Danielle decided to leave her boyfriend and just nine months later she was happily married. She and her new husband have two children now and are very happily married.

Cameo is exotic-looking and I notice she has an accent as well. When I ask where she is from, she tells me that she was born in Brazil and moved to the States as a young girl. She now has two young girls of her own. She has been in abusive relationships her entire life, most of which have also included alcoholism. Her question to Spirit was this.

"Will me and my boyfriend get back together again?"

It looks possible. We are asking you why you want to be abused again and to feel sad.

"That is not what I want at all. He can be very nice and he likes my girls. Do you think he can change someday?"

He can be very nice. He is, however, still an alcoholic and he does get violent. Even though he has been kind to your girls, in this time, you are teaching them that it is good to be with a man that hits you. You say he does not hit them, but they will learn that it is love to be with an abuser. So same same for your girls is being created in their future relationships with men. See?

Yes, he can change someday. Will he, is not for certain. You can get back with him when he quits this behavior. Yes? He will need the help of a professional to conquer this.

If you don't want to be abused and you don't want to be with an addict, then you are the one that must quit. Do you see that you are addicted to this substance of being with the wrong guy?

"I know, but it is hard because I still love him."

Alcoholics love their alcohol too. The addict, they quit because they don't like what it is doing to their lives, not because they don't still love, want, and feel a need for the substance.

You are addicted to dating this one and have fear of being alone. There is good support for you at Love and Sex Addicts Anonymous. You are addicted to being with someone bad for you.

Tristan is a sporty girl, looking as if she is right out of *Surfer* magazine. No makeup and sun-kissed hair and skin. She is usually perky and peaceful at the same time. Today she is shaken to the core. Her boyfriend suddenly moved out when she was at a yoga retreat.

Tristan's question is:

"Where did he go, why won't he talk to me, what happened?"

Dear one, we are so very sorry for your pain at this time. This one you have loved very deeply. He has always been moody and you know this. He does not verbalize feelings. You do not verbalize feelings often. He is left from you because he craves drama and would have you worry, but tells himself it is better because you don't care anyway. None of this is true but you know that when he gets deeply depressed, it is this way. He will not seek medical help we see. We have spoken of a Naturopathic approach to managing his depression, but you see he does not want that. For his own reasons he would rather leave you than allow change for himself. He has many things that haunt him.

"Is he schizophrenic? Bipolar? I really want to help him."

This is not for labels, but we do see, as we have told you, that he would be best in the care of a psychologist or psychiatrist. You do want to help him. However, you must see when you cannot help someone who does not want to be helped.

"I'm afraid he will commit suicide."

Yes, and you must understand that it is not because you stay or do not stay by his side. This suicide is something that will be his and his alone to save himself. You must not own this one's actions. You should report your concerns to family of his or to the suicide hotline. He does threaten in order to keep you attached, while pushing you away at the same time. Do you not see that he is unavailable for a full relationship just as much as a married man is not fully available to you? This is an unhealthy relationship and he does not sincerely want to heal at this time.

Jeremy is such a loving spirit. He first came to me when his relationship of seven years ended and he was deeply depressed. He and his new partner came to see me together. They are buying and decorating a beach cottage together. This time Jeremy wants to ask Beau if he will marry him. He also knows that he cannot ask this, without telling his own brother first. His brother and he have always been close except for one thing. His brother is homophobic, and everything about him believes it is not okay to be gay.

Jeremy asks:

"Beau and I are building a life together and we would like to get married. We are both very concerned about how some of our family might take this. Especially because I have not ever told my family that I am gay. I think my mom kind of might know or at least suspect this. I know my brother is not ready to hear this and will not be able to accept me. I love my brother and respect him. We have always been rather close and I really just don't know what to do about telling him. Can you give us some direction?"

You are assuming one cannot handle the truth and therefore you withhold the truth. Real truth is that someone cannot truly love you if you do not let them know who you truly are. You are ready to marry. Your family will deal with your news each in their own way. This is not your responsibility to decide what truth they can and cannot deal with. Do not rob another of the opportunity for personal growth. Trust that your brother and your mother are capable of love and capable of truth. Begin first with the truth that your preference in love is different than they might have assumed. Let them have time to understand their feelings and come to know the truth of you.

Do not expect them to embrace a wedding at the same time or perhaps divert some blame to your Beau. If you feel that your brother may need some support in accepting this information, you may wish to have your counselor present or we will be happy to assist with this.

Yvonne has been following a book called *The Rules* as a way to help her not to be so eager in dating and give away the farm on the first date. It has certainly helped her so far. Now she is asking this.

"So Mike just had foot surgery and is home, laid up and feeling yucky. I really want to call and check on him. But *The Rules* say not to initiate anything, just to let the guy make the moves. What should I do?"

Dear one, this is a matter of kindness. This is not chasing him. You are a kind person and want to show a kindness. It is very nice to offer some soup or a meal. Bringing a magazine or any small token to someone ill and housebound would be kind and thoughtful. This is someone you know and care for in this time. Perhaps you can relax and think of him as you would any other friend in need. This is not a case of you stalking him. It will be simply received as the kindness it is.

After years of being an intuitive channel and hearing spirit describe what it is like as a man, I think I am beginning to get the picture, or at least a glimpse of it. It still drives me crazy that they prefer not to ask for directions, but now I do understand their reasons. I am by nature very helpful to those I love. My husband and my boys are grown men and do not need me always to help them. They are fully capable of helping themselves. They in fact feel better doing things on their own. They want to conquer whatever they are up against on their own. When I give them advice and try to help them out of a jam they are actually hearing this: "She does not think I can take care of this. She does not have faith in me." What I think I am saying is, "I love you and I already know how to accomplish this better than you so just let me do it for you." It has been very hard for me to grasp that this is not the kindness they want, but rather showing them up and even removing some of the fun. The figuring out how to get out of a jam or conquer some obstacle is what they enjoy and take pride in.

*Do not help a man over seven years old
unless he has asked for your help.*

ROMANTIC RELATIONSHIPS

My husband had escorted a good friend of mine and me to a theater event. When we left the venue we took a different route to the car. When we reached the spot we had left the car it was not there. We were all confused as to how this could happen. My husband said not to worry he would figure this out. My helpful friend went to call the parking police right away and I asked her not to. I explained that Pete was very capable and liked to master these things on his own. She was sure she could get to the bottom of this faster or even get a parking attendant with a golf cart to drive us around looking for our car. She let me convince her to allow Pete to find the car in his own way. I just kept saying I know my honey can find the car. He always knows how to find the car. It did take perhaps twenty-plus minutes for Pete to get back, track his steps, and figure out what was going on. It turned out this parking structure had two mirror parking garages. One garage was labeled on each floor with different fruits. The other garage was labeled on each floor using different vegetables. We were simply looking for our car in the incorrect produce aisle! He saved the day.

Online dating, chatting, and flirting is quite a popular way that people are meeting. It can be common for someone to pick up an online relationship with someone across the city or across the country. The advice of Spirit is consistently this:

> *If you are feeling this is someone you would like to date, don't waste hours online before finding out. There are men and women who are using this as entertainment, and have no real intention to meet you. If you enjoy endless hours of communicating with people online you can continue to enjoy it. If, however, you are hoping that you really may have found someone you would like to meet, you will know enough by the third typed communication to move forward to meeting them.*

If a man or woman does not want to commit to meeting you after just a couple of written interactions. It is not real. Cut to the chase. Arrange to meet for a date or quit the texting. It is not a real dating relationship if you have never met in person! You can do a lot of getting to know each other online, but it just is not real life. You cannot walk down the aisle on Skype and have it be a legal marriage. For good reason.

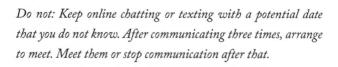

Do not: Keep online chatting or texting with a potential date that you do not know. After communicating three times, arrange to meet. Meet them or stop communication after that.

Be careful what you ask for. Have you ever said "I just want to get married"? There is no greater misery then being married to the wrong person. I know it can be very lonely alone, and I also know that being lonely inside of a marriage is even worse.

When you are dating, enjoy the process. You are learning about others and you are also learning about yourself. Enjoy discovering what you like in relationships as well as what you don't. Remember that you are whole, complete, and lovable just as you are. If a partner doesn't want to be with you it is about them and there is nothing you can do about them. Be honest with yourself about what you need and want in a relationship.

Don't date what you don't want. If this date represents an old pattern that you have quit, cut it off quickly and move on. You want just the right partner to share love and happiness, so don't settle.

You won't be attracting a wonderful perfect partner when your time is consumed, holding on to a just okay partner.

THREE

MARRIAGE, DIVORCE, AND PARTNERSHIP

I t is born into our nature to be together. We are a species that likes to mate and create family and tribe. In every culture I can think of there is a ceremony to celebrate and sanctify the union of committed love. In many ceremonies there is music and dancing, flowers, drinking, and feasting. The most extravagant is often the ceremony to celebrate the commitment of Love.

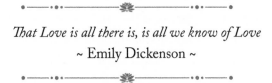

That Love is all there is, is all we know of Love
~ Emily Dickenson ~

Love and marriage can be so many different things in different relationships. To some it is security from poverty, or a partner for having children with. For many couples sharing life's highs and lows is the joy they want with someone. Some just don't want to be alone, or they step into married life for social, family, or religious reasons. Some want someone to grow old with and for security. I think it is safe to say that most of us choose committed love when we feel it will improve our lives. Otherwise we would avoid it, wouldn't we?

So why do we hear people say that marriage is hard? That marriage takes a lot of work? I am not at all in favor of these comments. I prefer comments that are positive in their core belief on marriage.

I know I am not alone when I say that I was even more scared when I decided to marry the second time. Why more scared? Because I knew how very painful divorce was and I never wanted to be in that much pain again.

I did get married again. I was able to say yes again because somewhere within me I still had faith in love. Those who get married or make commitments to love do so because they believe it will bring happiness. I had the advantage of intuition helping me and I was still afraid. Also when I was asking God what to do I received an answer that really helped me. **"Forever and always is a very long time, and it is pure bliss."**

At the same moment I saw my husband and me with family and friends celebrating a milestone wedding anniversary.

After nineteen years of bliss with my second husband, I can guarantee to you that love, joy, and peace are possible in marriage.

It is my wish for each of you that you will also receive a clear message of guidance for yourself when you need it most. I believe you will. Even knowing that I really did hear and see a positive message, my personal courage had to be summoned. I still had to summon courage to embrace marriage again. It is not quite enough just to develop your intuition. You will also need to trust your intuition and most of all have the courage to follow through and act on your intuition. I think we can all agree that hope and faith in love must be within us somewhere or we would not vow our love in marriage once, let alone again and even again. Let's face it, we **do not** really enter marriage expecting it to be more trouble than it's worth. Anything worth having and treasuring "Till death do us part" is certainly worth effort. I just prefer not to call it work. Instead I call it attention. We must invest our attention into anything we wish to preserve. Boats, homes, gardens, businesses, and treasures in the home all require effort to keep them in good order. If we quit caring for them they become deteriorated and we become disinterested. I really believe we first become less interested and then we begin to neglect. The principles of Feng Shui point out that neglected and broken items begins to decline even faster.

Feng Shui is the study of the environment and how it affects those dwelling in it. It is not necessary to believe in Feng Shui; it is simply an approach to making your environment more pleasant to enjoy. At every moment wherever you are, you are affected by your surroundings. There are places we prefer for relaxing that make us feel good and areas that do not feel good to us. A room with windows simply feels different than a room without windows. Feng Shui offers an approach to creating the perfect balance between people, places, and things.

When my husband and I were purchasing our recent home we consulted an expert in compass style Feng Shui. Compass style Feng Shui takes into account ley lines of energy in the Earth and polarities. Think about how much the ocean is affected by the movement of the planets. We are affected by the movements of the planets as well according to where we are positioned. The Feng Shui consultant explained that a home facing a southwest direction would give the most support to our particular partnership and finances.

We found a few homes and checked their position according to a small compass we brought with us. In the end we were interested in a couple of homes that did not face the directions we were looking for and one home that faced southwest. My husband asked for a reading and this was his question:

MARRIAGE, DIVORCE, AND PARTNERSHIP

"How important really is the direction our home faces?"

How important is the gender of your wife?

So, we purchased the southwest facing home.

This home will be very social and offer many friends.

Though life has still offered some challenges living in a southwest facing home, it seems to be good for us. We have been very content here for fifteen years.

Have you ever been in a home, maybe even your own, where the pets get more loving attention than the spouse? I have two little balls of fur that do nothing to help around the house, and never help with meals or income. Without complaint I take care of them, including their messy business. When I come home they greet me at the door like they have never loved anyone like they love me. They bark, twist, jump, and wiggle. I greet them too with equal enthusiasm.

Try meeting your spouse with treats after work, rubbing their back while you talk cute to them and tell them you just love them to pieces. A pat on the rump and then a walk together outside while you catch up on the day. Is your wife or husband worth as much love and attention as your pets? That is a great way to have a happy husband or wife.

Sometimes people play a game I like to call "Blame, Blame, who's to Blame." When this begins there are not going to be kisses and treats at the door and no tail will be there wagging either. Learn to verbalize frustrations and discontent in a way that communicates what you need from your spouse. Ideally learn to find a way to express what you need from your spouse rather than what is wrong with them or their behavior. Speak up early and you will find simple communication can prevent a great deal of discontent.

MARRIAGE, DIVORCE, AND PARTNERSHIP

Divine has often referred to a book called *Non-Violent Communication*. I found very helpful teachings in the book that have helped me to change how I might frame some of my comments. There are also books that can help you to have a disagreement and even an argument without ruining the relationship completely. I have experienced some couples where one or both are fighting to the death. Unless you really wish to kill the relationship you must learn to fight fair. Keeping in mind that you would like to be understood and that you do not wish to bring an atomic bomb in on your spouse and the relationship.

After a brutal divorce which I refer to as my "Near Death Divorce," I had lost a lot of faith in men and the possibility of everlasting love. Many people I have spoken to after divorce feel exhausted and doubtful they will ever marry again.

I hear everyone say marriage is work. As I mentioned already, I'm not a fan of this belief. Mass consciousness seems to be in agreement that long-term love is soooo hard. My belief is—why do anything that is so hard that it isn't fun and fulfilling? Then comes the blaming of men blaming the way women are and women blaming men. No gender or person is the whole problem, ever! If you find yourself blaming an entire gender for being the problem in relationships perhaps you would do yourself a favor by understanding the other half better. The gay and lesbian community can teach us that it isn't all the problem of flawed men or all flawed women. We are all flawed in some way and we are on Earth to learn and grow together. Let's let go of the blame game because, if it is entirely the other person's fault, you are helpless to affect change. We need to take responsibility for ourselves. If you are open to your share in the cause, seeing the part you played, a solution can be possible.

Why did the gay community fight so hard for the right to marry? Many reasons of course, but not because any of us really think love ever after will be a drag. We experience joy and fulfillment in love and we want it to continue forever. So we get married "till death do us part." Then sometimes something bad happens and we start wishing death would part us. We fall out of love. Do we really just fall out of love, or does it slip? I propose that if we can love our partner as ourselves we can make love last.

Imagine this scenario with me for a moment. You take off on your honeymoon with your new luggage filled with all your favorite clothes and beauty products. Your partner does the same packing, including all the best he or she has to offer, to begin this love adventure. The clothes get dirty, the tubes of cream and toothpaste begin to crumple from use. At some point there are souvenirs to mark this memory and that memory. By the time it is time to travel home you might be throwing things into different bags. Imagine a bag for dirty clothes, and the other reserved for clean. Personal products have merged as you share toothpaste and it might now be relegated to the same bag. You gather up the various items to stow them in suitcases while you make room for precious mementos. Now as you board the plane for home you have often mixed at least some of your baggage. It is no longer my baggage and their baggage. It is all **Our** baggage.

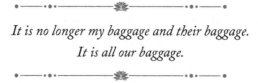

It is no longer my baggage and their baggage.
It is all our baggage.

Think of this as a metaphor for your life, from the moment you say YES to walking down the aisle. In other words, if the one you are marrying is a victim of abuse or perhaps an alcoholic or over spender, it is now your baggage too. I really mean for you to say **We** have sexual abuse issues or *We* have spending issues. *We* need to be cautious about addiction tendencies. You did not choose this person by accident. You knew on some level exactly what you were getting into and even needed it to complete a soul process of growth in this area. I didn't know this the first time that I married. It is very clear to me now that I had abandonment issues and I married someone who would ultimately abandon me. The ironic thing is that we usually blame and therefore do not grow forward after such trauma. Does this mean we should be afraid to marry our issues? Of course not. It does means that when it comes time to argue about something it is **Our** issue to work out together, and not our partner's problem to blame away. If you walk down the aisle and hold this belief to heart during your marriage you can have tender love forever and always, while learning to love yourself and another with even more depth than you thought possible.

My husband and I were newly married and he was very helpful. In fact he would come home from working all day and start picking up around the house or throwing in some wash. When I was single I had on my love list that I intended to attract a man who was a helpmate and I did. However as he would begin helping around the house, I observed myself feeling as if I was not enough. My old paradigm of the woman keeping all the house came up. When he helped around the house, I felt as if he was pointing out how unlovable I was, because I could not do it all myself. I kept telling him to go relax, play with the kids, I've got this. I'll get to this, just leave it. It troubled me to receive help as a form of affection from him.

Here is what was going on for him. His way of showing love is to offer acts of service. He was showing me great love with this service and I was discounting his love offering, by pushing him away. He felt confused that his love offering made me cranky. I felt inadequate and not lovable if I could not do it all myself. I got what I asked for in a helpmate husband.

Communication was the key for both of us to find balance in our new relationship. I am so glad I was able to communicate with him the inadequacy I felt when he helped around the house. Even better I was able to shift my beliefs and adore him for all of his help.

Here are a few questions asked by married or committed partners.

Jeff asked:

"Is she cheating on me? Who is it with? Why?"

It is true that she has been distracted by another. It is not her intention to be unfaithful, but it can become much more romantic over time. With this one she is feeling more loved, more understood, supported. See? Just a friendship but physical attraction is there too. This is her love language. You do not look at her when she talks. You do not really listen and you actually don't care to do this. Think if you are loving her and want to keep this relationship. It looks as if you do and you must give her what makes her feel loved. You are giving very nice things and working hard. This makes you feel very lovable, but it does not make her feel loved. See?

Janet requested:

"Tell me about my family"

Hello, dear one. You are really asking about your husband. Yes? We see he has turned his back on you. You are struggling with what decision you should make.

"Yes."

Dear one, it is clear that he is standing with his back to you and will not turn around. He has filed for divorce. You are not sure if you should keep trying. It is not a decision whether to stay in the marriage or not. That decision was made a long time ago. You do not love him. He does not love you. The decision is to move forward and create a better future for yourself and your children. You cannot single-handedly save this marriage and if you are honest with Self you just don't want to. You are financially scared. This is truth, yes?

"Yes"

One person dancing alone cannot make a marriage. It literally does take two to tango and he will not dance with you.

Mia asks Spirit:

"Does my husband love me?"

Yes.

"Is he having an affair?"

Yes, there is another.

"I thought you said he loved me. How could he be having an affair if he really loves me?"

We are sad to tell you that this love of yours has looked elsewhere for entertainment. He is like a little boy addicted to a video game. It has become a diversion for him. The question is of addiction, not of loss of love. Yes, there is precursor to his choosing this outlet. There is a story here in his past, but also in your relationship together. He loves you very much. We see that you are in love although very upset here. He will join you in counseling. You must arrange it, doing much leg work, but he will join you. He does want to be with you, if you can both forgive. We say both because you both have much to forgive each other, but also the Self. You see he has wronged his Self, his beliefs, his virtuous way that he sees Self. He will need to forgive himself for this as well as things in his past that he does not yet realize as part of him.

"How can I ever forgive him for this?"

Forgive the person, the soul that he is. You do not find that you can forgive the doing of this, and the betrayal. The book called Radical Forgiveness may be of help to you in this. It is also for you to forgive Self. Ultimately it will be to realize there is nothing to forgive. Only growth forward for you. You will in time create a much stronger and happier marriage. Believe it is so.

I don't think anyone on the outside of a relationship can truly understand fully the fiber that weaves through it. Relationships are living, breathing intimate beings only fully known to those participating in them. A relationship is an entity in its own right and when it dies there is mourning. Even if you are the one who initiated or wanted the breakup, you will likely feel a deep loss. What is being lost is often the dreams and hopes of what you believed the relationship would become. It is much like losing a loved one to death, in that you are losing your future with them and what they and you were to become together. For someone with abandonment issues it is common to feel these feelings of abandonment amplified. This can happen even if you are the one leaving and know that it is best for you to call it over.

Relationships are living, breathing intimate beings of their own nature, and only fully known to those participating and living in them.

Beatrice has been married in her words "forever," to John.

"Is my husband cheating?"

Yes.

"Can you tell who it is? Does he love her? Is this someone he really cares about?"

Dear one, we can tell you who and when, but that is not the question here. You are with this man for a long time and he has cheated before. Yes?

"Yes, a few times."

He will always have women around him. He has a great need for female attention. He needs to have his desirability confirmed a lot. He has been this way even when you were dating, he was married then.

"Yes, but that was different, because he was leaving her."

This may be so, however, the truth of him is that he will tell a woman, just as he told you at one time, whatever she needs to hear. He will most often have another woman, at least some of the time. You have known this and are always spying on him. He loves you but not only you and he is not capable of monogamy.

"Well, I do still want to be with him. Can't he change?"

Yes, of course he can change. First one has to want to change, and he does not want to change. He thinks this is just how he is and girls will always have to accept that. You have been very angry, but you have accepted it for many times over.

"What should I do?"

This is for you to decide. We can assure you he is true to himself only and has no intention to change. You can decide to stay or go depending on what you want for Self. He will remain the same throughout this lifetime.

Ivy is sixty-four years young and married her childhood sweetheart many years ago.

Ivy simply asks:

"Can you tell me what I should do?"

So much confusion. You are trying to make a decision staying, going, forward and back. And that is the worst of it, the not knowing what to do. Once you can be firm in your decision, it will be less traumatic. How can we help you with what you need to know to complete the decision?

"I want to know, I guess, about my husband. He has lied and I have forgiven him."

He lied and you have forgiven, but you are concerned about him still? You are not feeling you have the truth from him.

You have forgiven but not forgiven. Betrayal and hurt, it is one thing to forgive, another to regain trust. This man we see has cheated, but he is not a cheater. He has been faithful to your marriage for over thirty years. This is against his regular nature. He is very remorseful and he does still love you. This one is a victim of his own self. Almost like a little boy who says "I don't know why I threw the rock, I just wanted to." Right away you want to know the reason from him. But why would you throw a rock if you know it will hurt someone or something? You cannot understand how he could "not know" why he did this. How can you really understand that? No, you can't because you are a girl. But it is the kind of the answer you are getting.

What we want to say to you. Would a good reason for this behavior really help you? No, it would not. There is not a reason good enough. There is no reason we can think of where you would say "Oh okay. Don't worry about what you did then." There is no such thing, and there is no amount of clarity that could make this okay with you. You are asking for some clarity and honesty to back up a lie, and the honesty you are getting, well, it doesn't feel like honesty either. It is hedgy. You see him like he is dancing a bit, squirming a little. Every alarm in you and the back of your hairs are in alarm. You are smelling BS somewhere, and you are not getting the whole truth and that is the problem. You want to forgive, but to move on you have to trust and you cannot quite trust someone who will not give you the whole truth. Also, there is not truth that is a good enough reason to excuse what he has done.

To forgive is a decision. This decision to forgive is not based on what you get. It is to say I care enough about us and you, therefore I will set it aside. Even though it is a mark against you, I am going to set it aside and give you a do over. This is more honest in your case, because you really can't forgive yet. When you say to him I want to forgive you but I can't. I can't forgive what I don't know and there is still deception on the table. Every part of your skin is telling you this. Every part of you is attached only to what you don't know.

"I feel like it is making me sick."

It is making you sick. So our job here is to help you if you really want to forgive. You cannot keep this marriage if you cannot forgive. You believe you really can't fully forgive what you don't know, but we hope to get you to the point where you can. Let's keep you honest with yourself. You feel that if you don't know, you just can't budge off the subject, just can't let it go. Yet he will guard this truth as if it is his own life or death.

No good can come from the whole truth and nothing but the truth in this case. He is saying, "I don't know why I did this," and you can't believe he doesn't know why. Because if you threw a rock you would know darn well know exactly why you threw the rock. You can't quite buy that a grown man does not know why he has done such a thing. Well, those men can be funny animals, in that they can partition off the thinking. When he is saying I don't know it is because he cannot comprehend why he did this either and he knows he cannot give you a good enough answer. He can lie by omission better that he can tell you the truth and he feels he is saving his own life. He even tells himself he is saving you by his omission of the truth. Sad as this is to tell you, we do see a different way. We think you can forgive him if you know it won't happen again.

We think you can give him a second chance to love you honestly. But how do we get there to get the trust back? You are wanting to build the trust upon the truth, and he wants to give you a half-truth and say he can't remember the rest. This all makes you think something shady is going on. This all started with lies and now more lies. Unfortunately you will never get the whole truth. Even if he tells you all minutia and all of every feeling, even if he could. It would make it worse for you. Maybe you just don't want to watch the whole movie. Ever close your eyes in a movie? You may be watching a really good movie, but there is a part where they have just gone too far for your taste, and that you do not want to see. You are having to decide if you can forgive the whole thing. You can't forgive what he did and the betrayal and dishonesty. But you can try to heal and give him a do over. This only if you have certain changes and assurance to rebuild and keep trust.

"What about his job, his career?"

You know this has melted him, diminished him. There has been a sense of seeing him diminish lately through his working environment. You have seen his self-esteem dissolve. He feels also that you have been disappointed in him.

He could fight the bear to protect you, but he can't fight his own self-esteem melting. This is where we get to the real truth that he can't get in touch with enough to verbalize. There is a part of him that truly doesn't know that this has a lot to do with why he cheated on you.

When a relationship has ended, some people find they cannot stop thinking of the one they have lost.

Sherry asked Divine this:

"I have been divorced for six months and I know it is quite over. I know even that it is best if it is over. Still, every day I think about him and I cannot stop myself. I suddenly get the urge to text him and just share something. We used to drive each other to work. Now when I drive to work I keep thinking of things I would say to him. I think about him when I am brushing my teeth. I know it is not good for me, but how can I stop thinking about him constantly?"

Hello, dear one. This is a case of habit and we will tell you what is best to cure any thinking habits. Choose a new thought that is preferred and make a habit of the new thought. It is most helpful when any unwanted thought comes into the mind to put the hand up as you would to signal someone to stop. In this case it is you having an unwanted thought and you are putting up a stop signal with the hand. This can of course be done inside of your thoughts when you are in a public setting. Secondly, do not waste energy getting angry with Self for having an unwanted thought. You have had a very long-standing habit of thinking of this one and you have routines that have been habit together. The decision to quit is the first. Now think of something that is what you prefer to apply energy toward. Find a thought or affirmation that supports your highest and best good. Play it like a mantra in your head instead of the old thinking.

For you in this it will bring powerful change to you if you will please say the following. "I know and trust that I am attracting the best possible love partner for me right now!" *Each and every time you become wishful for your ex-partner say the affirmation. Every time you start to wonder what he is doing, say your affirmation. You are having a tendency to think thoughts about getting together again and wishing for this even though you know that he has remarried. This is not good for you. Replace these thoughts with your affirmation.*

In time the old thoughts will become less of an unconscious pattern for you. Take time to summon your new affirmation often so that it goes from being a conscious thought, to an unconscious habit. Your new affirmation has taken hold when it becomes the random thought that crosses your mind as unconscious thinking.

Nicole had a phone reading with me and this was one of her questions.

Nicole asks:

"After the last time I spoke with you a lot of what you said has already happened. I am getting ready to leave my husband. Well, I have left him actually. He responded in a way I wouldn't exactly say was favorable, but he didn't lose his cookies either, so to speak. He wants to be fair and have conversations and an amicable divorce. I just don't quite trust him and wonder if you have any information or ideas for me?"

Never trust anyone in a divorce. The loveliest person still wants the biggest half of the cookie and the generous way is to say here are the two halves—which one do you like? He is saying let's get along. I will divide the cookie, and I will assign the half that is your share. He is actually more fair when you let him cut the cookie and give you half. When you question him too much he gets a little bit more controlling. Even nasty. So we will lay out both pictures. He believes he can cut the cookie in half, dead center, but his hand won't quite let him do it. See? More if you can keep kindness toward him things can go smoothly. When a kid divides a cupcake, same thing happens. There is always a bigger half and the cutter wants it!! Engage very friendly; he does have more need to be in control than you.

"Yes. I think so."

He is more inclined to cut best halves when he cuts. You can start with the half he gives you. Say thank you for taking charge of all this. You both know he is the only one that will have to be in control, but you can thank him anyway. Thank you for taking this on. Thank you for working this out. Thanking him for his work on this, even though you know he would not allow any other way. You still thank him and say you are a good guy. I am happy and proud of us that we can go through this so smoothly. I also know you will understand that this part is really like a business decision and I hope you will be the man I know you are and understand that I would be stupid not to have a lawyer look at it. I do appreciate how you cut the cookie so carefully.

After you have a lawyer look at this and become aware of whatever guidance they tell you, and also if there is anything important for you, you can suggest changes. Then you say all right, all well and good, and by the way there is this one thing. Maybe you didn't think to write it down or whatever, but I want it. Maybe you assumed I would not want any of the music. But I do and so we need to address that. Basically you have said to him it is okay to me that you have control. He does believe he is being fair. He will appreciate credit for that and this helps to keep everything nicer between you.

It is our preference that you start with a mediator if you can agree to this. It looks as though mediation can assist you while keeping a peaceful environment.

Not all marriages are meant to last, and not all can be saved for this reason. Sometimes the love and the lessons are completed. Some couples cannot seem to be completely done. The torture of divorce can be the gift that keeps on giving. The pain of divorce and lost love can continue if it's over...but—It's Not over!! By this I mean when one or the other of the partners will refuse to move on. Many have come to me because their ex-spouse keeps harassing them in one way or another. Some ex-spouses keep believing, wrongly, that they can save the marriage, all by themselves with their personal willpower. Some people just can't forgive the wrongs or the fact that someone could get over them. Some manipulate the other through the children. Please seek professional help if this is happening to you.

Relationships are a chance for learning all the way along. Before jumping into a new relationship or rebounding into it, Divine always advises healing. Spirit recommends a few different options I have noticed. Some of the most common advice is Spiritual Counseling, Ministerial Counseling, and Psychotherapy. Some of the types of healing that have been most recommended are EMDR, hypnotherapy, and vibration or sound therapy. Please do seek out some form of healing so that you can grow in your soul and attract happier, more fulfilling relationships in the future. Understanding the part you played and learning to forgive yourself and your partner. Perhaps seeing a pattern in relationships that you can heal from and overcome. When you do this you can move on to better relationships in the future.

For some couples the healing of the relationship may have another motivation. What you don't learn in this lifetime will come back again so you can learn it. Be kind to those you are in relationship with. You may be seeing them in the future. If your issues are quit unresolved and volatile you will have an opportunity to make amends. To end peacefully may also be a way of avoiding this same go around with this same soul, and similar issues, in another lifetime.

Do try to love your partner as you love yourself.

FOUR

THE GIFTS OF FAMILY AND FRIENDS

Family and friends are our most treasured relationships and some-times they cause us our greatest grief. We love them so much and want very much to be loved, appreciated, and accepted by them. Sometimes we have to participate in family settings with people we actually don't like. I've heard it said "You can pick your friends but not your family." And isn't that so true. Still, family gatherings are more fun for all when everyone gets along.

You will likely know your siblings longer than anyone else you will know in this lifetime. If you are natural best friends, lucky you! If, however, you are opposite personalities or don't care for each other, you might want to think about what is best for you. Do you want a harmonious relationship with your siblings, and if so, what can be done towards deepening the good feelings between you? Sometimes it is necessary for your own survival to distance yourself completely from a family member. Make a clear decision one way or the other and make strides in that direction.

This from Megan who has plenty of good friends. She feels a hole in her heart ever since her parents' divorce, which divided the siblings. She says, *"Somehow it's never been the same."*

Megan asks:

"How can I create a better relationship with my siblings?"

It is true that you have little in common with them. They are living very far from you. With the sister, this one is in need of your friendship, as well. It is simple what to do. It is less simple perhaps in the doing. First we see with the two of you that if you will communicate often, you will be much closer. It is not that you must have a deep and meaningful relationship. Frequency is what brings you closer to each other. Because you only talk a couple of times a year it is impossible to know the day-to-day of her life and then it feels that you do not really know her. In order to know her you must increase how often you communicate the little day-to-day feelings and experiences.

First, it is good to tell her what is on your mind and heart about wanting a more meaningful relationship with her. In this way you are telling her, I would like for us to be closer. I would like to chat more. I will call and text more often, just to keep in touch.

Weekly is the minimum to connect if you wish to know each other closer. Today this is made much simpler. Send her a photo of your new shoes. Don't hesitate to ask, what color nails should I get today? Include her in your day-to-day life in small ways, even the mundane, and the silly. Siblings who are close share often but not necessarily deep stuff. It is that when something big or deep is going on you have created a safe and familiar relationship within which you can share. She has a very different life than you do, but you have background in common. You can contact her with a memory, just to say "remember when..."

You also have two brothers.

"Yes"

One of them is trouble for you. He is trouble for himself too. When you are around him you feel guilty because you don't know how to help him. What you do not accept is that you have nothing to do with his problems and cannot help him without hurting yourself. In reality you cannot help him at all, except by not helping. You have been thinking to have him live with you. Yes?

"Yes. Well, my husband is against it, but he, well... What is your guidance?"

This one is a troubled soul and he will not change coming under your roof. He is not safe to have around your children. You have a very happy and healthy home, and it might seem that this would help your brother. In this case, however, it would put strain on the marriage and children. These children are your first responsibility and the marriage of your children's parents.

Also you do not do well with him when he is around you. His effect on you is deleterious in every way. This would be damaging to your family harmony without being of help to him.

You do have one brother that you can be with and enjoy. He does seem to be able to offer help to the other brother, without getting pulled down himself. He is a very busy sort of guy and it's less easy to get a return call from him. He does love you, but he doesn't really see a need to get closer to you. Send him updates, rather than calling. Call your sister-in-law or keep with her on social media. The relationships with them are comfortable and casual. Don't expect much closeness with them at this time, except when you are physically there visiting. It is important to visit them or plan a trip together yearly if possible.

They have too much business in the day-to-day commitment to their own offspring, and may seem to ignore you. Try not to feel hurt, but rather to understand the love for you is there. They would come to your rescue if you needed them. They just don't have a desire to spend time sharing life, day-to-day with you.

There is not a person alive who can truly be an island. We are meant to be with other people, some of us need more contact than others. Following are two readings about time together. The need each of us has for alone time is a real need in each of us, and it is different in each of us as well.

Sabin called me from the Southwest for a phone reading. She was in urgent need of an intuitive reading because she is staying with family, and there is tension and hurt feelings. She has just arrived for a family visit and she has planned to be with them for one month. Sabin herself is going through a transition time and some personal turmoil.

She has been there less than one week. She is already feeling very angry, short tempered, and isn't even sure why she is feeling this way.

Sabin asks Divine this question:

> "I really love my sister and her family and I don't know what is happening to me. I keep thinking all of these really ugly thoughts. I don't know how to describe them and maybe I am just misinterpreting, but it feels awful. I am not sure if these thoughts are coming from me, or I am picking up the thoughts of others outside of me. Can you tell me what I need to know about this?"

THE GIFTS OF FAMILY AND FRIENDS

It is very valuable that you are getting in touch with yourself and your feelings. There are feelings within you of anger. You are feeling cranky and agitated with so much energy going around you, because of the intensity created by so many people. Even though these are loved ones, some of the children you hardly know. Also you have become so much more sensitive in the last two years. You are empathic more than previously. You are not used to this much togetherness and you are feeling rattled. Your family is feeling your temperament and they are wondering why. They are going out of their way to dote on you and make sure you have everything you would want or need. They are feeling your tension and that you are trying to distance yourself or avoid them.

"I know this and I feel so guilty."

You need time alone, Dear One. One of your core issues then, you could say, is that you want to please people. You are trying to please them with maximizing minutes with them. You are betraying your own need to crawl inside your own self and regenerate. You think of yourself as a friendly and gregarious person, and you are acting cold, quiet and rude. This makes you angry at Self.

"Yes."

You are needing time alone to reset the body battery. We see that you are trying to push through to please others, but what is happening is this. You are getting very tired and stressed. It is much better to explain that your need for a little alone time is greater than most perhaps at this time. Also that it is no reflection of the love you feel for your family. You want them to know that you will take a bit of time for yourself instead of trying to be around them constantly. You will be happier in your socializing with them when you are feeling better. In order to save them from your cranky self. LOL.

Asking for their understanding is kinder, you see. The other way to get the space you need has been to get grouchy, and then no one wants to be around you. They avoid you, and leave you alone. Either way, you get what you want. We prefer not hurting family feelings.

It is quite acceptable to turn in early for bed. Give yourself an extra hour to read, journal, meditate or just about anything alone that gives you peace. This you know about yourself and that it has nothing to do with how much you love someone. It is just a matter of too much energy going out into the room even to the best most loved among them. You need time inside of you to regroup.

Some people can be extraverted all day and then into the night. It is your structure that you cannot do this. It does have some to do with being empathic. Especially for the fact that this being empathic is a rather new development within you.

We are aware that you often need a break in the middle of the day and you cannot go ten hours of people. So in the middle of the day you say, "I need to go lay down and put my feet up for a little bit." People understand a nap and do not take that personally. It is your business if you sleep during your nap. Either way, nap or not, you do need to shut all down and go within. This is a way to do that.

There are also certain days when you will be out and about with no space for a nap. At these times we have a suggestion that may sound a bit humorous. Go to the bathroom, and let this be your safe haven of alone time. You may even wish to tell anyone in your company that you may be a while. You can sit and relax with the walls close to you and be alone for some peace of mind.

A mother of four children came for a reading. Her name is Alice and she began to get weepy even as she was sitting down and getting comfortable with a cup of tea. This spontaneous weeping often happens simply as people enter the powerful healing energy of my office.

Alice is concerned about her oldest child, who is now seventeen years old. She has been crying and is overwhelmed with his change in behavior.

Alice asks Spirit:

"My son is so grouchy I cannot say anything right. Ever! I feel bad saying this but I can't wait till he leaves for college. I'm very worried about him. He stays in his room on his computer and really only comes out to eat. When he does emerge he is terse and tense with the family. Is he involved in something bad or what? What can I do to help him?"

Dear One, this is normal to worry about your son. It is hard for you to know what is bothering him because he will not say. He is very much stressed right now. He is figuring out what he really needs to be doing for himself, grown up life is coming fast. He is not sure he knows what he is doing. He is more comfortable sharing these thoughts and fears with others his own age. They joke about their fears indirectly to relieve the stress.

He doesn't want to need your help, but is afraid that he sort of does need your help. He is overwhelmed with school and finals. He is overwhelmed with his girlfriend who is not happy he is going away to college. He isn't sure if he is feeling enough of a grown man to go away to college. At the same time he wishes he was off to college already, because he feels too grown up to be living with Mom. In his mind every word that you say is like nails on a chalk board.

He is very difficult to be with, so that both of you can welcome his leaving, when the time comes. He is very effectively pushing you away so you will leave him alone, and let him grow up.

This is very much a phase of growing up and is quite similar to the growth period that takes place when a child is two to three years old. A two- or three-year-old is learning that they are not their mom, and that they have a mind of their own. When you say come this way, the toddler wants to go any other way just to exercise their independence. It is a time of many meltdowns and tantrums because they are not able to accomplish the things they envision. They become aware of tasks that older people can do, and are not yet able to command their bodies to do everything they want to do for themselves. They see big kids doing things and they can imagine in their mind doing these things, but then the body at two years old cannot quite do them.

The teenager does not want to "need" his parents, and still does need them, to pay bills, drive the car, give permission, etc. The teen feels grown up and ready to "not need" the parent but in reality still needs them. Imagine how frustrating this is!

One of the most helpful things you can do is quit telling him anything. No homework reminders and certainly no reminders to bring sweatshirt or cash. No more advice on how to do this and that, he does not hear it anyway. He hears nails on the chalkboard. Better for him to be angry at Self than at you.

THE GIFTS OF FAMILY AND FRIENDS

He does hear you if you say words that reassure him of your faith in his adult capabilities. Let him know that you know he can do the job of conquering his world.

He will learn his own lessons much better for himself. He will prove you are right if you have told him he can conquer his life. When he has forgotten something like money, and experienced the result, the lesson will stick with him forever. Do not try to save him from suffering, or you will both suffer from your over parenting. You can soothe and comfort if asked, which you usually will not be asked to do.

"He has been complaining that I won't let him grow up."

Yes, and to him it feels then that you don't believe in his ability to be grown up. Let go, Mom, and let him fall or fly like an eagle. He is feeling that you have no faith in him. If you do not have faith in him, then he is not sure how he can have faith in himself. It would be rather insulting, as if you told your spouse to bring a warmer coat or when to wash his hands. You have done a fine job raising him. Time to let him fly.

Let go, Mom, and let him fall or fly like an eagle.

Here comes the bride. Her name is Gabi, which is short for Gabriella.

Here comes the question.

Gabi asks:

"What can I do about not wanting to invite my aunt to the wedding? My mother really wants me to invite my dad's sister. She and I had a falling out many years ago when she took my dad's side in the divorce."

Hello, Dear One, there is the smell of springtime on you with raspberries and we see many flowers. Wedding is to be a happy time and so often it is stressful. We would like to say this. You are in the position where you can make peace in a family.

Always think of what your wedding will symbolize. A wedding should symbolize Love, new beginnings, and family. With this also, it should be a symbol of forgiveness. Without forgiveness no family or marriage can last. You have the chance to be all of these beautiful expressions on your wedding day. Never do you want to start a new life with the harboring of old grudges.

This client showed up with a very tragic story. Her brother had passed suddenly and for unknown reasons. This was 1991, so many years ago, and I had never tried to get in touch with someone who had passed over to the other side. She asked if I would try to see if he could be reached and so I did. This is what he shared through me during my trance.

"A swarm of hornets was after me. I was not thinking and I dove into the window and broke through the glass. Next realization that I had I was trying to explain to Mom why I dove through the window, but then I realized that I was not alive. I was observing myself sprawled over the back of the sofa. It was a really weird awareness at that point!

"I just want to tell you I am happy. I want to tell you I am sorry I was not kinder to you, my sister. I know that you needed me to understand and to help you. I did not care and I let you

down. I hope you will talk to me now. I will listen and help you all that I can.

"I want mom to look on the shelf over my bed to the box there. Look under the box."

His mother looked and found a note/poem that he had written for Mother's Day, which at the time of his death had been just a few more days away.

Heather asks:

"I am completely at a loss about what to do for my mother. She doesn't want to move from Iowa to California, but I can't take care of her there and she is really starting to need care."

She is frightened to make a move, this is true. She has no family to care for her there but she does have lifelong friends and her church. Everything there is familiar to her. There is comfort for her in the familiar. Same dentist, doctor, market and all give her comfort just because they are familiar.

"I know and it is really hard to think of moving her away from the only home she has ever known. At the same time, there is no way I can move there. My husband's job is here and the kids are in middle school and high school. I have been trying to get back there every month to visit and help her with doctors appointments and all."

Dear One, we know you are in pain with this. You love your mother. You need to know you are doing enough. Yes, you could do more if she lived near you, but this is not for her best at this time. She still wants to feel independent and to stay in her home.

"Is she safe in her home?"

She is safe in her home for now. She stays well physically for some time; however, it is getting to be a problem with forgetting. She will need other housing in about eighteen months time. At which time she can come for a visit to California and stay with you.

"Will we need to move her to a rest home or adult care or something?"

Yes, this will become necessary at some point. When this comes about she can have the choice to live in an elder care facility in her hometown, or move in with you. You will offer to her that if she moves in with you it is temporary and she can go home if she at some point wants to. You would prefer she move in with you and this is a hard choice for her. She will be best able to handle the transitions if she can live in your home for about a year, little more maybe. Then she will need a facility because you cannot care for her at home.

At this time if she is already in California with you the transition to a care home is not as difficult on her. If she never moves in with you and she goes direct from living on her own in Iowa to a care home, she will prefer close to where she now lives. This is not the best because those friends that would visit her become fewer and those become less mobile to visit her as well. She will ultimately be happier with you and her grandkids visiting her. She can come for a long visit with you and then she will be happy with you. After a year of this she can make the decision to stay permanently. She cannot decide to move in with you in total at first, so for her sake you offer only a long visit. Only after she can experience this for a while she can realize she would be happy living with family.

"So you are saying that maybe a couple of years from now she will need to be in a care facility?"

Yes.

"Thank you, I feel so much better about this now. It feels good to have a plan for easing her into this change."

Jeb and Veronica are in my office to ask about a car accident that took place when they were on a double date with their best friends.

Veronica asks:

"We are in a horrible position with friends that we have known for many years, in fact Jeb and Steve have been best friends since childhood, and I have been great friends with his wife, Ann, since Jeb and I started dating in college.

"Okay so the problem you know is that Jeb was hurt very badly in the accident. Jeb has had four surgeries so far to rebuild his crushed cheekbone and broken jaw. We have no idea how much more he will have to go through and we have thousands of dollars of medical bills. Our insurance is billing their insurance and it's not like we even have a choice in this. That is the only way to get this paid. Our insurance won't pay until after they have sued Steve and Ann's insurance. Steve and Ann will not speak to us. Our families have been close all this time as well and it is a problem for everyone. The whole thing is set for trial and it has completely ruined our friendship."

Yes, Dear One. This is very sad and still you have no choice. Insurance is in place for these types of situations and they will do things their way. It is not personal to your friends, but they are taking it personally. They feel that you are suing them personally and blaming them. They are hurt by this and they are embarrassed that it implies to everyone that they are wrong.

"Is there a way to save our friendship? Is there some other way we could be handling this?"

No, it is sad to say, but you are not people in this insurance dispute but rather clients of each company. Each company is wanting to get the best advantage for their business investments. You have done your best to explain this to your friends and on some level they know that you are not doing this to be hateful to them. Still, they will not be able to speak to you. This friendship as you have known it has been changed permanently. What you can do for the best of all concerned is to send love to Steve and Ann and to the families. Even you can send loving white light and prayers of love to the entire court and the insurance companies. This you can do and keep doing. Stay in a loving place with your friends even while they cannot love you, and even while they do not want your love.

"This is awful and you are saying we are just helpless in this."

We are saying that you cannot change the insurance process and you cannot change your friends' perception of it at this time.

Prayer is not at all a helpless position. It will make powerful movement for your friends to eventually make peace.

There are a lot of stories I could share on these pages that would show the tender love and the deep pain that family and close friends can bring. I hope you have experienced the gift of love in your life. Most of us have also experienced betrayal from a loved one or friend.

When pain and betrayal is served to you from a good friend or loved one it does seem to cut so much deeper. We expect that the world at large might not always be on our side, but we count on family and friends to always have our back.

When deception and betrayal come, do try to ask your Higher Self for the guidance and strength to understand the deeper lesson. Learn how to forgive them, not for their sake, but for your own.

I don't know where my mom got this quote but she really made an impact on me when she said it. "Hate is like an acid, it burns the container it is in." My husband, being a man of science and engineering, never really endorsed this quote. He says this would not happen, as the acid would just be put in an acid-proof container.

"Okay, sweetie, take that up with your mother-in-law," was my response along with a giggle and a wink. I'm happy my mom and hubby enjoy each other so much that I can make these jokes.

Oh well, either way, it was great for making an impact on me as a child, and you all get it, right?

I also remember my Sunday school lesson, when my teacher said, "Vengeance is for the Lord" and explained that we were never to be vengeful.

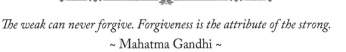

The weak can never forgive. Forgiveness is the attribute of the strong.
~ Mahatma Gandhi ~

We give friends and loved ones more of our intimate selves and this gives them more that can be used to hurt us. Without sharing, however, it is impossible to feel truly close. To love completely is the only way to feel completely loved. Look at it this way: if someone only knows you looking and behaving lovely, they really do not know the whole you. If someone does not know all of you, they can only like or dislike what they know. Isn't this the reason we want to put our best self forward when we meet new people? We all want to be liked. That is universal.

It is those really close friends and family that we allow to see us when we are down and out. When we are sick and gross and look a mess, they are the only ones allowed to come over. The fact that they know the down and dirty, not so pretty side of us, and they still love us. Well, isn't that the gold and silver of friendship and isn't that what we all really want?

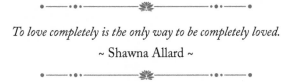

To love completely is the only way to be completely loved.
~ Shawna Allard ~

So there is a bit of risk involved in love and friendship. I prefer to call it trust, and, a surrender to that trust. This I know about myself, and that is, that I only let someone know my secrets if I trust them to hold them dear enough, not to hurt me with those secrets. That trust we endow our friends with is also where we often give them the fuel to burn us. Yes, there is risk involved. Friendship and love are risky, to be sure. I believe the greater risk is not to let anyone in too close. You will never know how much they might have loved you, or what a great friend they could have been. You might have a great ride or you might get burned. I guarantee neither will happen if you don't let anyone in. I think to live without relationships that dip into the depths of our core is to not fully live.

I have been betrayed by both family and close friends. There were a couple of times I thought it would nearly kill me. But in each case I learned a precious lesson.

I will risk it all again. I know I will be greatly rewarded with either painful lessons, or maybe this time—just love and loyalty.

FIVE

HEALTH AND SPRITUAL HEALING

We all want to live a healthy life and die peacefully in our sleep when the time comes. I often get asked why we can't control this. I have asked Spirit this question and so have numerous clients over the years. The answers vary because we all have differing outlooks, beliefs, bodies, etc. So clearly there are no one-size-fits-all answers.

Ideally we are a perfect balance of our bodies, minds, and our emotions. To live in harmony we need to balance all three aspects of this beautiful trio. It is easy to focus on the body because we see it in front of us day in and day out. When we are in front of a mirror, it stands boldly in front of us. When our body hurts or is unwell, we are totally aware of our discomfort. We are not often as intimately aware of our soul and mind, so they can more easily get ignored or neglected. Yet mind and spirit are certainly of great importance to bodily health.

Health is always a case of the Soul manifesting a body, mind, and spirit picture that culminates from all of our experiences, and related beliefs about those experiences, over all of our incarnations. From the realities that we believe we create our world and our experiences.

That being said, you cannot so easily change a subconscious belief just because you decide to. Deeply stored in our soul memory is everything that ever happened to us in all of our many incarnations. Especially when things happened that affected us deep within our soul, our soul memory captures it in the vault of experiences. In this soul vault is all of our many experiences through the body, mind, and emotional levels as well as our beliefs about those experiences. It is as if they get "locked up" in us. The trick, so to speak, might be in finding the key to your lock for release and freedom from pain and illness. If you are sick right now you tend to desire a cure, right now. Western medicine offers instant relief and while that sounds enticing the real cure usually requires a deeper look into Self. Especially when looking at a repeated illness or injury tendency, it may be helpful to look in the past.

There may well be a disturbing and unresolved incident in your past, even a previous lifetime. What is a major trauma for one person might not have an effect on someone else. We expect someone returning from a gruesome war experience might have some PTSD (post traumatic stress disorder). It is also perfectly normal for a person to evaluate a situation from their point of view at the time of crisis, a child, for example, may make a decision about their body from a point of reference that is not necessarily accurate at the time. If this is not cleared up, the skewed perspective will continue to influence all decisions and can affect illness for all time forward. For best results in health and healing we have to address all three areas of body, mind, and emotion in the past and present.

Bodies today are required to live under some crazy levels of stress. Our fast-paced worlds are bombarded with information and a sense that we should always be moving and doing. At the same time, much of the information we chase after and manage is available to us in a sitting-at-the-computer lifestyle. The stress is very real in the brain and in the body, but normally our bodies are designed to run fast if we are under attack. We use our brains nonstop and many are neglecting the physical body and the spiritual body. We all know we should get regular exercise and some spiritual or at minimum quiet time.

All bodies need to run fast, physically exert and sweat. All souls have needs too. They need time in meditation, nature, quietude, and spiritual reflection. Bodies need healthy natural foods. Minds need to think and create, learn and expand. Most of us certainly understand all the above, but it sure can be challenging to create and maintain a balanced life.

If your life needs to be brought into balance, look to correct that first. When seeking help look for a professional that realizes the entire body, mind, and spirit connection. It is vital to any healing endeavor. I will share several stories that I hope will speak to something you or a loved one might be dealing with.

I have never been seriously ill, ever. I have always considered myself to be very healthy and I still have a strong immune system today. Until ten years ago I would have said I was structurally sound as well. However, over the last several years I have experienced several bone, joint, and structural breakdowns in my body. I remember offering to take some of my dad's karma many years ago when he first became paralyzed. I have wondered if these physical difficulties were part of that offer? Either way, I have known them as karma and tried to endure and learn my lessons accordingly.

I have considered the fact that I played hard in my twenties and crashed a lot on the ski slopes, the mountain bike trails, and the ice arena. Back then I thought I was invincible, now, not so much. I do see where many of my physical challenges come from injuries in the past that have become worse with age. I believe that some of my injuries could have been less if I had honored my body with gentler care over time. I sure had fun being adventurous and I wouldn't and can't change the past.

I am lying in bed as I type this chapter because I am healing from surgery on my foot. In the past several years I have experienced a lot of various structural problems in my body and undergone several surgeries. I had a lot of pain before each surgery, or I would not have chosen surgery. For all of you wondering why I did not try more natural approaches, believe me, I tried all of them. Of course I included prayer as well. There was a good bit of pain as I recovered from the various surgeries. This all put a strain on me emotionally, and squeezed me to grow even more spiritually. I have seen many people including me learn lessons through pain that they refused to learn any other way. Maybe that is the reason for some of our pain and illness. I know some pain is frequently related to karma. Astrological charts can reveal aspects of a person's health too. We can see in someone's astrological chart if they may have entered this world with a predisposition toward injuries and accidents or illness. There must be a purpose for this.

For many years before this time I had been offering spiritual healing sessions and Reiki. I enjoyed this part of my profession and found it very rewarding. I knew that it was helpful to my clients and they were experiencing great results.

During the trials of all these pains and surgeries, I decided that it just wasn't right for me to offer healing if I could not heal myself. Who was I to help others heal if I was such a mess? Well, a lovely human angel told me something very dear to me and I want to share it with you as well. She said:

"If only those doctors and nurses who have never been ill were allowed to practice medicine, and all the psychologists could only serve if they had never suffered from emotional pains, we would not have any doctors, nurses, or psychologists."

Wow! This was a deep truth for me. I know I am actually better able to help others after some of my personal experience. I guess doctors, nurses, mental health professionals have also learned a great deal from whatever physical and emotional experiences they have had.

I have gone on to help a lot of people, even while I was trying to get to the root cause of my own challenges. I have always told my clients that it is never as simple as a broken bone or cancer, there is always a spiritual, emotional, and karmic connection as well. In the early 1980s when I began saying this it was a lot harder for people to see it. I am happy to see how this has become accepted and many are looking at the body, mind, emotion, and spirit as the connected organism that it is.

If you or a family member struggle with a serious ailment, or as my dad did being a quadriplegic (paralyzed from the neck down), the question of their karma may come up. I know people have said to me before, do you know or can you even imagine what your dad's karma must be? It used to bother me to think my dad must have committed some terrible violation in the past and this was the cause of his present life's karma. Our struggles and lessons are uniquely and individually designed for us. Be careful of judging and instead always be willing to assist someone in need. We are all here to learn, and *none* among us has always been a perfect saint in our many incarnations. Someone that is challenged with the unimaginable task of navigating life with mental or physical disabilities can teach us many things. Seek to understand your own lesson rather than what theirs might be. They are on this planet with us to learn with us, grow, and to be our teachers.

Please be patient and compassionate when you see someone ailing. It is a blessing to all if you can offer assistance. It is a blessing to no one to point out that they have brought this on themselves or maybe even deserve it.

HEALTH AND SPIRITUAL HEALING

If you are struggling with any illness or setback, maybe you have felt like, why me? I know my dad, who had been all muscle, loved to do gymnastics and skiing, must have felt this way. He was only thirty-five years young with a wife and three children to support. He had plenty of living to do. I'm sure he asked *why me, God?*

When my pain overwhelmed me I certainly asked the questions, Why me? What have I done? When will I be done suffering? I got no answers to my questions, except to surrender to the pain and ask how I can serve others. My struggle has been nothing compared to some, and still, all that I could personally bear at times. More importantly, my experiences have made me a better, more compassionate and empathic healer.

I would like to offer some words of comfort regarding the suffering of body, mind, or spirit. What I have heard Divine say about this has varied from person to person. One theme seems to stand out in each case. When everything is sunny and jolly it doesn't seem to encourage humanity to seek God. A large percentage of humanity will seek understanding, spiritual growth, and God when they are experiencing struggle in their lives. Perhaps it is because we refuse to learn the easy way. If we all expressed through love and kept to the good habits we know, would suffering lessen?

I first began to offer hands on healing in the early 1990's because two of my clients asked me to do a healing on them. They both said they had received a healing when they came for a reading, and they wanted to return for more healing. Of course I told them I had no idea what I was doing, but we would ask Creator to come on through me again, as that is the source of all healing anyway. According to them it had value and they both continued to come for healing.

I studied Reiki after this and received my Reiki Master degree. I found a spiritual teacher that had been offering healing for many years and I studied with her. I joined the Holistic Nurses Association learning and sharing with nurses and other healers. I gave instruction on seeing the aura and my style of healing as well.

I attended a three-day retreat class offered by Barbara Brennan, author of *Hands of Light*, in New Mexico. I met a dear friend at the Barbara Brennan retreat. She was financially able to attend the classes held at Barbara's school back East. It was out of reach for me at the time, both financially and because I had two pre-school children at home.

I prayed and prayed to God, please to make some miracle possible that I might attend the classes back East at the Barbara Brennan School of Healing. This was the answer I received:

Who do you think taught Jesus, and many others?

I also received instructions on how to study her courses at home and through Spirit, if I wanted to. I did want to and this is what I learned to do. I found out when the courses were being offered. I went into a deep meditation and joined the classes throughout their offering, by out of body travel. I (my soul body) would leave my physical body and instantly be in the classroom. It was an experience of "sitting in" on the various classes.

I was also guided during trance to "travel" through books in the libraries around the world. I could feel myself passing through the pages, absorbing the knowledge in each book. I want to explain that it was an absorbing that felt like osmosis rather than some photographic memory. I had a deep experience of each book I entered in a fullness that was more than mere reading. It was a sense of energetic Truth embedded in my Knowing, rather than my conscious memory of words.

I know it sounds "way out there," and it does to me too, even as I type this over twenty-eight years later. But here is the really cool part. My girlfriend came back after her first year of classes at The Barbara

Brennan School of Healing. We got together to share and do some healing on friends. She was amazed at my progress and asked me.

"That's extraordinary! How did you learn third year stuff ahead of me? Really, that's the stuff they teach in the second and third year. You have to tell me what you have been doing!"

When I would do readings for someone in need of healing, various offerings might come through that Spirit felt would help them. I heard many suggestions ranging from, hypnosis, guided imagery, massage, Feng Shui, affirmations, and journaling. I wanted to study and learn these healing tools as well. I allowed Divine to do the healing through me, but I still desired that element of knowing what was being done. I studied everything I could.

What I found most interesting was that healing and intuition show up in my astrological charts, both Vedic and Western, as my calling in this lifetime. It is my dharma (a Sanskrit word for duty, calling, right living) to heal and counsel intuitively and the blessings have been there all along. My person, or ego, needed education and proof to allow myself to believe it, to surrender to it. Now I just show up next to the healing table with unconditional love in my heart and say,

"God bless this one before you with healing and all that serves their highest good, and I'll do as you direct me. Let all who come in contact with me (by my words, deeds, or my presence) be blessed, healed, and brought closer to Thee."

It has always been my prayer and mission statement, and you will see it posted in my office, as well as every goals board I have ever created.

More and more people on the planet right now are feeling a calling within them to be healers. We are entering a beautiful age, where more souls can heal and raise others to a new level of awareness. If you feel called to be a healer, it is already there to awaken when you feel ready to allow it. Ask the only real healing energy, God, to come through you to help others heal, and ask to be guided to your right modalities and teachers. Remember that when you have a great passion for something, the Universe has that same passion for you as well. I am happy to help you in any way that I can.

I would like to share a story now from a long time ago. I don't remember her name. She was having stomach issues and no one could tell her what was wrong.

I got her relaxed on my healing table and began to scan the energies of the body. I was attracted to her left knee. As I was allowing healing energy to pour lovingly forth, I asked her to look into that knee herself with her mind's eye. As she continued to breathe in and out, with her consciousness in her knee, she began to cry softly.

I asked her to describe what she was feeling.

"Shame, and it hurts really bad. It didn't hurt when I came in."

"I know, ask your knee what it might want you to know, at this time."

"I remember when I hurt this knee getting out of the car. We were in a car accident. My mom yelled at me to stay in the car. She is really upset and I know I have been very bad. I feel ashamed. I feel ashamed and my knee hurts."

"What is going on in your life today that you are feeling ashamed about?"

"Well, I really don't want to tell you, because I'm ashamed. Okay so, well, I made a bad mistake and it troubles me every day. I don't think I can make it right so I just keep it inside trying to figure it out. Do I have to tell you for you to be able to help me?"

"No, but you do need to do something to be able to make it right and forgive yourself. You need to be able to speak it to someone. You came here because your tummy was in a very bad way. That is where you are holding the guilt about what you have done wrong. I will continue to transmit healing. Just continue to breathe into your knee and you will know when there is peace there.

Some time passed in silence as the healing continued. Eventually she said:

"I know what I need to do."

She was then able to tell me about the recent shame. She also got in touch with three other times of similar instances where she was feeling ashamed. Her decision was to tell the others she needed to talk to and to share her guilt and shame.

When we met the following week she shared that her tummy was fine the minute she made her decision to share. Further, her truth in sharing turned out to be a healing for one of the people she shared with. So in a way my healing was only a way of observing her pain, being with her in it without judgment. Sometimes we just need validation, to be our truth, and still be loveable. Sharing our truth can heal so much, but we often do not share our guilt and shame, because, well—we are ashamed. We fear we will be judged.

Do you have a secret you can't imagine anyone would understand? Do you have secret pain that you are afraid to share, for fear of rejection? Who can you talk to that might be a witness to your pain without judgment? Could that help you to let it go? Perhaps even help someone else to let their shame go? Find someone you can trust, you will feel better.

Cancer is a tough one, right? We hear that word and something inside of us cringes with dread. Almost everyone has experienced this for themselves, a friend, or a loved one. There is plenty out there about how to eat right to avoid cancer and that is not my department. It is also not really my place to tell people how their thinking this or that got them to my table. Once someone is here and they are wanting "It" to go away, we are just addressing the cancer and the present energies.

When I see cancer energetically (or in my mind's eye), I see it as a darkness, often a weed of sorts. I acknowledge it, but I do not dwell on "getting rid of it" in any way. I see beyond the ailments, whatever they may be, to the Truth. I see the Truth of the pure and perfect health within them. This is key to being a healer. You must be able to see the entire human essence as already perfect and whole. The perfection within us created by God already exists. The illness is a road map that shows us where our beliefs departed from Truth. Seeing the wholeness, whole health, and wellbeing as created in perfection is the only way to experience true health. Healing is the true power of thought and the power of prayer in action, affirming health. So a healer should never be trying to "get rid" of anything. We only help you to discover the cause behind disease so you can release it.

When we are pure and have perfectly balanced connectedness with Holy Spirit at the spiritual level, we are not our bodies. When there is illness, pain, cancer, or any malady in the body, that's just it, it is in the body. We are not our body, but rather our soul. It is the body expressing something, but it is not the Truth of the person. It is an illusion of the Earthly existence that is being seen and experienced.

Keeping all this in mind, it would still make me feel a little hurt, if someone told me, "It's not real, you just created this in the mind." Would this hurt your feelings?

Now that we understand our ailments can originate from karma, as well as our thinking related to our experiences, we get to not only feel sick or hurt, we also feel guilty for creating it. People tell me they feel sick with guilt and that they must have caused this illness. Okay, I get how that comes about, but dump that thinking! This thinking and the guilt is only making you sicker!

HEALTH AND SPIRITUAL HEALING

Guilt, shame, anger, etc. are just the tip of the iceberg that is often at the root of illness, particularly cancer. So please don't waste a precious minute feeling guilty about being sick, hurting and angry.

I will share with you one of my favorite healing exercises. Divine has taught me this exercise and I often find it helpful for people with cancer.

Exercise from Spirit:

You need a sky with a few clouds for this exercise.

You are going to ask a cloud to disappear and it will.

Sit or lie down in a comfortable position for meditation.

Find a cloud that is all alone or a small cloud that's part of a group of clouds.

Get in touch with the most spiritual experience you can remember.

Recall how that made you feel. Be that Spirit-filled feeling.

Focus that Love of Spirit you feel right now.

Focus this on the small cloud.

Feel the small cloud and you and Spirit as one.

Ask the cloud gently to effervesce, just melt away, back into nothingness.

Do not try to "get rid" of the cloud at all. What we resist persists. Right?

You are relaxed, not doing anything, acknowledge the cloud with your Love.

Keep holding a loving focus on this cloud, as you allow it to release.

Allow fifteen to twenty minutes.

As the cloud is fading you want to say "Thank you" or "I release you in love."

Was that easy for you? Fun, right?

If you didn't do it easily, you were trying too hard and it didn't work. Be patient with yourself and simply try again. Remember to relax and "allow" the cloud to release.

This lovely young girl came to my office to seek healing. She was quite up front about the fact that she had a tumor and the doctors wanted to surgically remove it. Surgical removal looked like a good idea to me as well, and I told her as much. The thing is she knew it was not right for her to have the surgery.

We proceeded with hands on healing. Through me Spirit directed her through many exercises of energy, vibration, focus, and visualization. I saw the tumor energetically disappear completely. On her next visit the tumor was back again, with some changes to its density or vibration, but still there the following week. Each time she came to see me she was able to make a shift in the tumor and when she could no longer find it we would end the session for that day. I was very impressed with her focus and her ability to conquer this tumor.

I have seen many cases where Spirit suggests surgery to remove cancer. I want to address a question I often hear that I think is a really valid question.

"If Spirit can heal anything, why surgery? Can't we just make it go away? I mean I want to learn whatever the lesson is."

Many of you may have been thinking this very same question.

What I know to be true is that, yes, we can make anything disappear if we have faith, and perhaps learn the related lessons to help us release it. We absolutely can. I also know that sometimes we need a bit of a head start as in removing the fast spreading disease AND simultaneously addressing what brought it about in the first place. In other words, some situations are going to run out of time before the body, mind, and spirit that has created the situation has time to reverse it. So we go forward and do what we can to heal the mind, karmic, and spiritual lessons, while also asking the "cancer cloud" to disappear. This does not mean you should turn your back on modern medicine. It was created by God as well. Everyone's situation, body, mindset, and every vibration of who they are is different. You can only choose for yourself what is right and go with your own gut feeling.

As to the lovely young girl, one day I called to see how she was doing and ended up leaving a voice mail. When she returned my call she told me she had checked into the hospital. She had been suddenly overcome with a pain she could not handle and thought maybe it was appendicitis, so she went to the emergency room. There she met the perfect doctor that listened to her concerns, the perfect surgeon for her.

I know she learned and healed a great deal in the many weeks of refusing surgery. She followed her intuition and didn't want the surgery.

Then at the exact moment she needed, she met the right surgeon. This moment in time felt right, and this surgeon felt right. She said yes to the surgery and now she is cancer free. Through our work together she has also neutralized the original cause. We cannot know why she needed to wait, but I firmly believed in her personal intuition.

She shared with me a concern that perhaps she had made the wrong decision at the beginning, not to have the tumor removed. I see that it was not the right timing or the right surgeon in the beginning. She needed to have some experiences and healing before she was ready.

What happened with all the hands on healing? We moved and removed a lot of blockages, emotionally, spiritually, mentally and physically. I believe some of what we did was to make room for her to attract the right surgeon and be ready to accept the surgery. The reasons for the creation of this tumor and the related lessons to be learned can be complex. She followed her personal intuition to achieve a complete healing.

Again, each person has to go within and make the decision that is right for their body. I know it can be very difficult if a loved one makes a decision that you disagree with, especially if their life is on the line. You may have a very clear idea of how you would like them to handle it. This is a good time to trust in prayer to help them and perhaps to help you accept their decision.

Just when I see certain patterns that I "think" can be explained, I remind myself not to "think." Thinking is not my job here. Do you know a person with an emotionally closed heart, who is dealing with coronary blockages? It might be tempting to assume they have closed down their heart. I am reminded how unique each one of us is. There is often more to it than that. There are stories of adoption and foster homes and broken hearts that can contribute to difficulties of the heart. There are also karmic reasons, DNA, and just poor eating habits.

Most often Spirit will suggest stretches for the chest combined with mental and emotional exercises. Yoga and tai chi and chi gong come up often as advice for healing. What's so wonderful is that the person will usually say, "Oh my gosh I've always wanted to do that," or "I just started doing that." They know what they need and I just remind them.

When there is heart trouble, frequently there have been many broken hearts for this person along their soul's path. By this I mean not only this lifetime but past lives as well.

I believe the healing ability rushes through each and every one of us all the time. When someone sees you are hurting and gently lays a hand on yours, you feel just a little better. When a child is hurt, the mom will touch the boo boo or lift the child into her arms. Dads and other loving figures do this as well. We know we are healers and it is often as natural as breathing for us to offer healing. I like to think of it as love glitter, and I sprinkle it everywhere I go.

When our daughter was six years old she would routinely heal the children on the playground. I happened to be at school one day volunteering and walked onto the playground. Her little friend scraped a knee and was crying. She ran up to our daughter for healing, and I learned many children would do this. My little angel had seen me healing loved ones and evidently took it as what we just do when someone is in need. She bent down, closed her eyes, placed her hand on the knee for a moment of prayer. Then she said, "There you go. All better now," and they bounced off across the playground as if nothing at all had taken place.

In our household it is quite common for me to ask a family member for healing or prayer. In this modern age we think nothing of texting a request when needed. This brings me to distance healing. Yep, just as real, and just as easy. Trust in your Creator, by whatever name you use, and when you think about it, why would distance matter to the Creator of the universe? Right!

Some people visit me for healing or balancing of the chakras. There are seven main chakras that run from the base of the spine to the top of the head. Chakras are a spinning energy or life force located in specific areas of the body. Every chakra has a beautiful sound, color, smell and feel unique to each of them.

For an illustration and more in depth information regarding chakras, please visit my website at https:/www.DivineKnowing.com

The seven main chakras are the centers in our bodies in which energy flows.

Blocked energy in any one of our seven chakras can often lead to illness, so it's important to understand what each chakra represents. Here is a quick summary of each chakra.

1. ROOT CHAKRA
Located at the base of the spine.

Color: Red

Represents: Our foundation and feelings of being grounded. It is associated with issues of survival such as fight or flight, money, food, shelter, and physical survival.

2. SACRAL CHAKRA
Located in the lower abdomen about two inches below the navel.

Color: Orange

Represents: Abundance, well-being, creativity, pleasure, and sexuality.

3. SOLAR PLEXUS CHAKRA
Located in the upper abdomen.

Color: Yellow

Represents: Feeling confident and in control, self-worth, self-esteem.

HEALTH AND SPIRITUAL HEALING

4. HEART CHAKRA

Located center of the chest at the heart level.

Color: Green

Represents: Love, joy, and healing.

5. THROAT CHAKRA

Located at the throat.

Color: Blue

Represents: Communication, self-expression through verbal as well as written.

6. THIRD EYE CHAKRA

Located in the forehead just above the eyes.

Color: Indigo

Represents: Intuition, imagination, and wisdom.

7. CROWN CHAKRA

Located at the very top of the head.

Color: White

Represents: Our ability to connect to Creator, spirituality and bliss.

A chakra might become blocked or bogged down for any number of reasons. Experiences of powerlessness might affect the solar plexus. Trauma around speaking up for yourself might cause you to restrict the throat chakra as a way to protect from over sharing. Often abuse that is physical or sexual and has us wanting to run away can cause problems in the base or second chakra. The one most people can relate to is the feeling of a broken heart. Have you experienced that feeling after loss of love where your heart feels literally in pain? It can feel constricting and aching, tight and gripping. Many people have had this feeling of the heart chakra closing down from loss of love. Much like the pupil of your eye constricts and becomes smaller in bright light, the chakras can constrict and limit the energy flow through them.

There are times when it is beneficial to our health and protection that we feel a sensation in the various chakras. It can be a form of intuition that an area of our being is under threat from another. You may have had the feeling of being watched or a sense of instant dislike for another person. Where do you feel the sensation? Notice how body language speaks louder than words. When you feel threatened by someone you automatically cross your arms to protect your energy and your personal space.

I adore crystals and gems and their use as healing tools. I've been collecting rocks, and gems since I was five years old. I collected them because I thought of them as incredible unique works of art, and I love them. I guess that might be the way you think of a friend or a pet. Maybe you love their personality and expression, you just want them around. That is how I feel about crystals, rocks, and gems. I also use them in healing, because they do have a quality or vibration, unique to each stone. The energy or personality of a stone often matches the energy I wish to increase or decrease for my client. They may not have life as life is currently defined, but when it comes to moving energy, it's there and that is the unique quality I am attracted to.

Gems and crystals act as conduits for healing by encouraging the flow of positive energies from the stone to the body, while allowing the body to release negative energy into the stone. For thousands of years, precious and semi-precious gemstones have been utilized for healing of mental, physical, and spiritual ailments. They can still be useful today as an additional technique along with more traditional medical practices. The use of rocks and gems in healing has been utilized to cure ailments, protect against illness, disease, and injury. They are especially potent in supporting mental balance and stability for spiritual purposes.

Nikola Tesla, a renowned inventor, electrical and mechanical engineer, physicist, and futurist, declared all things in the universe are forms of energy. All things in the universe are forms of energy with their own unique frequency and vibration. He proved how certain forms of energy can alter the vibrating resonance of other forms of energy.

Obviously ancient cultures were not aware of any scientific basis for the use of crystals, but numerous cultures have long utilized stones in healing, protection, and spiritual practices.

The Native Americans understood the vibration and energy in nature and used various tools such as rocks for healing. In Roman culture, gems and crystals were often fitted into jewelry and talismans for enhancing health, attracting desirable people or things, and for providing protection in battle.

The ancient Egyptians utilized crystals in many ways, including burying their dead with crystals and gems. Egyptians carried and wore various stones and crystal jewelry for health, protection, well being, to attract love and foster sex appeal.

The word crystal comes from the Greek word for ice, as the ancients regarded crystal as pure water that had frozen so deeply that it would always remain solid. The ancient Greeks associated iron with Aries, the god of war. Hematite, an iron ore, comes from the Greek word for blood. The word amethyst means "not drunken" and was worn to prevent both drunkenness and hangovers. Greek sailors were known to wear a variety of amulets to keep them safe at sea.

In India, crystals have long been used for healing emotional and metaphysical imbalances. In Hinduism, the Kalpa tree, or wish-granting tree, is made out of crystals and precious stones. The use of healing crystals is documented within the Hindu Vedas. Composed in **Vedic** Sanskrit, the texts constitute the oldest scriptures of **Hinduism**. The Vedas reference numerous stones and their healing abilities. Sapphire is thought to bring astuteness, clarity, and mental balance. Jasper is said to bring harmony, sexual vitality, and balance.

Stones and crystals were also used in ancient Asia and are still frequently used today. Crystal spheres were commonly used in Japan as a fortune-telling tool. The Chinese used crystals in various healing methods and crystal-tipped needles were used to enhance acupuncture.

Jade has been highly valued in China since ancient times, known to have been used since before 3000 BC. The Chinese considered jade to have strong healing properties and was considered a stone of concentrated love essence. Elsewhere, the Maoris of New Zealand wore jade pendants representing the ancestor spirits, and continue to believe that the stone is lucky. Jade was recognized as a kidney healing stone in South America as well as China.

All over the word, turquoise has been worn to give strength and health and jaspers have long been believed to provide strength and calm. Amber has been the most widely used in talismans, and amber beads were discovered in Europe, dating back some twelve thousand years ago.

If the color of the rock matches the color of the chakra you are wishing to energize, you are on the right track. If the ailment or disease needs to diminish, think about colors that diminish. Warm/hot colors diminish too much cold, and cold colors will be best for reducing fever and inflammation. Too much fluid in a joint? Don't use a color that represents water such as a blue or green stone. If you are unsure of the correct stone, use clear quartz crystal. Looking to heat up a dull area, try a red stone. Anger and anxiety can be soothed with

HEALTH AND SPIRITUAL HEALING

peaceful or cool colors such as shades of green or blue. An easy way to know which stone or gem to use is to trust your intuition and intention. The person in need of assistance can easily pick out a stone for themselves, as they will be drawn to it.

Herbs, vitamins, essential oils, and homeopathic remedies are all wonderful tools that enhance the healing of the body. For guidance on the appropriate use and dosage of these it would be wise to hire a professional. Dr. Bach originated the Bach Flower Remedies in the 1920-1930's as a safe and natural method of healing that can be used to enhance your personal wellbeing. Acupuncture, massage, and chiropractic certainly have a place in the natural healing of the body. I have heard Divine recommend all of these and more during various readings. Healing is a very individual decision and I can only speak to the methods I personally use with intuitive healing. Whatever path you choose for your healing, find someone highly qualified to help you through the process and trust your own intuition as well.

Every time I come to the healing table, I thank God and the person before me for allowing me into the miracle that is life. I am there to hold witness, not to judge or think. The minute you "think" you know what is going on is the minute you need to "think" about not "thinking" anything at all. So whether it is cancer or a hangnail, I never know what will come up. I am just the open flute for Spirit to play through, the same as I am when I channel. I am so grateful every day to be blessed with the gifts of intuition and healing awareness, to facilitate as I do. Nothing more than just be myself, stand in, as a bridge between Heaven and Earth.

You are a healer too. You can do this too.

SIX

CHILDREN AND PARENTING

Children are God's gift to us, so that we might feel a glimmer of the love God feels for us, his children. The immense love we have for our children is an example of the love the Divine has for us. We are loved deeper and more completely by God than we can comprehend. To feel the depth and immensity of God's love for us is only possible in deep meditation, an out of body experience, or a near death experience.

When I held my newborn child in my arms I felt a love that was at once complete and unconditional, with an all-encompassing intensity and to a degree that felt both completely blissful and painfully deep.

I will share what I have learned from twenty-nine years as an intuitive and parent of three children. I have answered countless questions from other parents. I have a few experiences of my own as well, having raised three kids, all of whom have turned out to be great individuals, probably in spite of any mistakes I made as a parent.

Has anyone else noticed how much easier it was to know what to do with everyone else's kids, before you had children of your own?

They come in with a big bunch of personality too! There may be a case for nurture vs. nature, but any parent will tell you that children come in with a certain personal nature of their own from the beginning.

I know we are only their caretakers for a while when they are young. They never really "belong" to us. The reality is, in another lifetime, it could easily have been our own little child who played the part of our caretaker. Who knows, they may have been old Uncle Ben or Aunt Sue, the very ones who raised us up, and have since passed on.

I do know this, however—they sure feel like MINE. I would die for them, fight for them, and do whatever it takes to guide them. Even past the point when they say, "Stop already, Mom. I got it the first time you said it." I repeat myself a lot. I don't repeat myself because I think they are dense, I do it because I can't remember if I said that already. I'm scared to miss something they need to know, or anything that might protect them in life. I know how well people learn from their missteps and mistakes and that we all make them. However, I just can't help wanting to cushion the world for my children and protect them from pain of any sort.

I realize some of you may have experienced abusive parents and endured screwed up parents as well. Possibly the pain and shame of incest, as I have. Even the best of parents are only human and we can all blame our parents for something. Childhood experiences as well as raising children have huge potential for igniting our vulnerabilities and helping us to grow. As a parent, even if "being the best parent you could be" has been your fervent prayer since they were born, your kids will have an opinion of what you could have done better. Even if you have never been a parent, you have been someone's offspring so let's try to understand it's the hardest job ever invented. Some do it with love and tolerance, and some just can't. Some folks really didn't mean to have kids, and some just didn't mean to be mean. I hope you grew up surrounded by love, which makes it a whole lot easier to offer a

CHILDREN AND PARENTING

loving environment to your kids. Either way, don't judge the job until you've walked several miles, over a decade or two, in your mother's high heels or dad's work shoes.

Most people who come to see me ask about their children or their own parents.

When I married Pete he adopted the two children from my first marriage. We felt complete and totally happy. We decided to have just one more if we could. Well, in truth I requested a two for one special, as in twins. I became pregnant shortly after we married and we were elated. I nicknamed the baby cheesecake because I craved cheesecake during my pregnancy as if it were the only food on the planet worth consuming. After five months of pregnancy I had a miscarriage. We suffered deeply the loss of this baby. I was so consumed with grief that for days I simply could not get out of bed. I felt that I literally could not make myself rise. We gave the baby project a rest for a while.

When we were ready to try again I was forty-three, and because of my age we were concerned I might be running out of time (biological clock). We sought help from a fertility specialist. We needed only a little help from a fertility doctor, but still I got a glimpse of what many couples endure just to conceive a baby and the devastating loss that many experience month after month.

As I shared with you, I did request twins. This is what God had to say about that.

Everest

"You want me to name the baby Everest?"

No, Mount Everest.

"Oh, don't people die climbing Mount Everest?"

CHILDREN AND PARENTING

Exactly! A chocolate chip cookie is amazing, but too many will make you sick.

"OH... so no twins?"

LOL...silence on the line.

When I became pregnant with our third child we asked Divine about the names we were considering for the baby. Each name has a vibration and I think it makes total sense to seek out a numerologist before you name a child. I believe this to be useful and even critical, but we didn't have our children's names looked at by a numerologist before we named them. For whatever reasons we were bound and determined to use the names we used and that was that. I had a lovely name picked out which I was very fond of. One of the older kids voiced their opinion along the lines of, "No Way." Let's face it there is so much in a name that there are certain names we dislike, and that is that. Nobody but me was excited about the name.

My husband and I had a reading about which name would best suit our little cherub. Guess who showed up? None other than the proud, would-be owner of this new name. When we asked him about the name I was thinking would be great for him, he simply said:

"My mommy can call me whatever she wants to. I will define my name, my name will not define me."

We went with the family favorite as a name anyway, but how cute our little guy was. He is still true to this personality. He is happy to please and go along with what is, but at the same time, he is clear and headstrong about who he is.

There is a lot to a name whether you are naming a person or a business; if you are renaming yourself, or taking the last name of a new partner—these are all times to check the numerology of the name.

When I am doing a reading and someone asks a question for or about someone else who is not present, it is the name of that person I ask for. From the name I know who we are talking about. Even with all the Steve's in the world, somehow the name will connect me to the one in question.

Parents always ask questions about their children. They desire happiness and good health for their children, and they want to know they are doing a good job as a parent.

A couple showed up for an intuitive session with their four-year-old in tow so I could meet him. They knew he was very gifted and special. They also noted that he would say weird things about people he knew before in another life. He acted different than other children. Not in a bad way, just different. He told a neighbor once, "You were my mom before, don't you remember that?"

They had many questions but all basically the same essence. "What can we do for him and with him? What can we teach him, when we think it will just be him teaching us anyway? What is the best school for a child like ours?"

Your son is very gifted. There will be more born like him at this time because the age of the Earth and people of the Earth are ready for greater teachers.

At this time, he is just a child for you to raise. He is yours to raise, because you can, and because he chose you for all that you will be as a parent. Even the ways that you may come up short as a parent, your child has chosen this too. You have chosen the lessons you will learn through your experience of this exact child. This is true for all parents and children.

He does need a smaller school and less chaos around him. Surround him with people who share your values. He can be very emotional and feels things very deeply. He does come in

CHILDREN AND PARENTING

with great knowledge and many lives he has evolved to be here. Let him grow and he will. Do connect him to music, to churches, to architecture. This will support him. Love him as he is and this is mostly how any child will flourish.

Many children at a young age show signs of intuition and talk about seeing people the average person cannot. When my oldest son was very young he used to comment as he was looking at the ceiling, "Aren't they pretty colors" meaning the angels on the ceiling, he told me. At one point while sitting in the car behind my mother he said, "Nana, why do you have those pretty colors on your head?"

Once a very devoted father of two boys, raising them alone, came to see me. He is raising them alone because the mother is bi-polar as well as addicted to substances of various types. She is not reliable in her personality and has put the children in danger. She has been unable to mother them most of the time and is presently in an institution.

Marcus is the father's name and here is his question.

"I love my boys and they come first for me. Can you tell me if they are okay and will they have scars from their mother's mental illness?"

There is some scarring, yes, you could call it that. Keep in mind that they are affected by all that surrounds them. Some is more fun and some not. All, however, is formative for them. What affects them most has been the solid foundation they feel from you. You have given them a very good sense of themselves and their self-worth. They know they are safe and solid in your

CHILDREN AND PARENTING

love. There is some effect on them regarding relationships with women. Therapy can help them to have a balanced view of what is right love.

"I have a question about that actually. I have been dating this woman and we are in love. Her name is Camille and I just want to hear what you have to say."

She is a lovely and lively one, yes? She and you do have a rather special bond and you do feel love for her. What you have chosen, however, is another "not fit for motherhood" kind of woman. In this case you know she does not want children in this lifetime.

"Yes, and I guess that is a large part of what I am wondering. Can I marry her and would this all work out okay? My boys come first and that's absolute. Will she be good with them? I don't really need her to be their mother. I am doing all of that. But she would be in the home and I just want to make sure everyone would get along okay."

Dear One, we see what is in your heart. She is not right for the family. She does not want to be a family. She is very selfish about her needs and you would always be pulled in between her needs and the needs of your boys. She has no ability, as well as no desire to develop such, to share the piece of cake. She does not want to share you, the spotlight, or any other such. You cannot have her in the house without your boys getting an impression of womanhood from her. They will also further develop their own value when it comes to a woman.

There is another woman for you. She is for the boys as well. You will find that you cannot love someone who does not love

145

your boys. You will have difficulty with Camille as soon as she wants what is best for her, and not the boys.

This is important for you to know here. You can have it all if you want to. Seek a woman who loves all of you, and all of you is the boys too. This woman you will meet has not had children of her own, dear one, and yours are her gift of motherhood. Your boys are as much a blessing to you as all of you are to her.

Janice came for a reading, because she was troubled by her eight-year-old son. She told me there was a very good chance he was gay. This is her question.

"Look, I just want to know if my son is gay or not? Please just level with me because I'm okay with it either way. I just mostly want to know how to be a good parent to him and how to guide him."

He has come in with this tendency and will most likely grow up to realize himself as preferring the company of men. His dad is not okay with who he is, not even without considering his gender orientation. Dad picks on him in subtle and not so subtle ways. He is a passive aggressive bully, this husband of yours. The dad is making it impossible for this boy to relax, as he cannot please his father. This alone will not make him gay. It will cause low self-clarity, low esteem for Self.

We see that you are going through a separation from the father at this time. Yes?

"Yes"

You have a question about him? The husband.

"Well, I have been wondering if I should try harder to save the marriage?"

He, your husband, would like this, but you don't like who he is as a person. You see him as cruel and sneaky so this will not be possible for you to save a marriage with someone when you dislike their qualities in total.

"Ya, that's kind of what I've been thinking. I know."

We are sorry for your loss. It is, however, a big breath of relief for the son. This dad does try harder and do better after the divorce, which is good for you to know. Something in the dad changes. One of the changes is that you seek counseling for your son. As the child changes, so does the way the world treats him. Even the way his own dad responds to him and treats him will change to some amount.

His bedroom is hard for him and he sleeps in your room? Yes, this will be the case for one year and more. This is normal for many children at least thru age six.

The energy in this child's room is greatly improved with moving the energy. Some living spaces can get stuck energy and this room has a problem with this. The child also has trouble letting go of issues he is stuck on. A simple solution is a ceiling fan which is left on at all times, with just a slow setting. Other remedies can be music playing or a wall clock that has a pendulum in motion.

Linda arrived at my office with questions about her daughter.

"How is my daughter Sylvia doing?"

CHILDREN AND PARENTING

She is very much at peace and relaxed. She is worried about you.

What happened to her? Was it intentional?

Not intentional to have this outcome, no. It was an accident.

"How did she get the heroin then? And why? Was there someone trying to harm her?"

She was given a gift not in order to cause her harm but rather to insure the continuation of profit for the gift giver. She had no conscious intention to utilize it but accepting to keep it with her. She was happy and content with her strength in overcoming her condition of addiction. It was not planned that she would use the heroin, but there it was and she simply decided to "try" it. Of course this was a lie to herself, and that is how addiction works. She overdosed on the same amount which she was most recently familiar with using. Because her body had become less tolerant, the amount was too much for her system. She does want you to know that you did everything right. She was happy again. She does say it is difficult to find a truly watertight baggie and water will find its way in. Much the same heroin was impossible to keep out, it found a way to seep back into her life.

This couple came for a reading about several issues in their marriage as well as for one of their children, Sarah. Mrs. Tibit asked Divine this question.

Mrs. Tibit asks:

"We have been having a very hard time keeping our marriage together, and although we try not to fight in front of Sarah, I know there have been times when she probably heard us. She is thirteen now and she is very aware when we are not getting along.

"I know she has been having trouble with some of her friends at school. Some of them have been very mean to her. She has been trying to blend into a different group of friends. We are very concerned about her well-being. What can you say to us?"

Dear Ones, this lovely one is very troubled at this time. It is wonderful she will talk to you and still, she is more troubled than you know. She has been hurting from your loss of love, but more she is concerned of herself right now. She has lost her friends because she did not agree with them and she was picked on for this. Her trying to change friends would be good except the group admitting her to their circle is not a positive. They are a troubled group seeing the negative side of all things. They experiment and she is not willing to stand up to them and risk the loss of friendship again.

"I saw scratches on her arms. Is this what you mean? Something didn't feel right. She said she just scraped her arm on some bushes. I knew I didn't feel right about this being truthful, but I didn't know what to do. Is our daughter cutting herself?"

This is correct the cutting. Worse is the cutting to feel included. To feel alive in a way. She is also under other pressures from this group and made to feel she must prove she is one of them. Her new group of friends is very much not good for her. Removal is difficult. She feels abandoned and without friendship. Little in the world is as awful as no friends and no group when you are in this age group.

149

We recommend a therapist for her with a specialty in teens. We can recommend the one we see will be good for her. She does need to change schools or home school for the remainder of the year. This to disrupt this friendship lifeline she is holding onto. For this child of yours there is a group from church, once a best friend there, which the ties have withered. These can be reestablished simply by returning to the youth group at this vulnerable time, and while she is removed from her current school.

"Is she going to be all right then? Is she really messed up?"

Not messed up, Dear Ones, confused and looking for a place to land. You see, if you are in an airplane and you need to find solid ground, that is of utmost importance and you must find this solid ground at all cost or you will perish. This your daughter is feeling that she must find a place to fit or she will perish. You could say, she is trying to find a place to land on solid ground. It is as real to her as with the airplane, because without a group she feels she will perish. She found a place to land and she landed in a bad spot. Too far to hike out, see? Give her a better landing spot and she will take it. It is easier said than done, but you can do this.

CHILDREN AND PARENTING

Peg asked this question during a phone reading.

"My husband and I really want another baby. I am so scared that I just can't do another pregnancy. I was so seriously sick with morning sickness, all day long for the entire pregnancy. At one point I had to be admitted to the hospital. I had to quit work and I couldn't even take care of myself with the first pregnancy.

"I have a healthy baby girl now, but she is a handful. There is no way I can have morning sickness like I did before and take care of a toddler. So my question is should we adopt or is there a chance I won't be as sick this time if I get pregnant?"

You will have morning sickness some, and nothing like before in your pregnancy. You will feel much better this go around. Adoption is a fine option for you as far as being a parent a second time. This process, however, it is so long to receive the baby that the emotions are too hard for you. Most lovely path for you is pregnancy again. You will be feeling better this time by far.

I saw Claire before she got married eight years ago. I had the honor of doing spiritual hands on healing while she was pregnant with her first child. She told me that the nurses were all shocked when she emerged from her room the very next day walking around like she had not just had a C-section. Claire felt completely fine the very next day after major surgery! The power of hands on healing is truly miraculous.

Now they are trying for a second baby and she has some questions.

Claire asks:

"We have been trying for eight months to get pregnant and nothing. First of all, can I even get pregnant, or did we wait too long? Also should we get help with fertility?"

Hello, Dear One, you are still fertile, this is absolute. Something is going on with your cycle and the fallopian tube is not open too much on one side. It is true that you are older and so are the eggs. Not as many juicy ones. We do see that you have a

CHILDREN AND PARENTING

151

chance to become pregnant over time of the next six months. It is also very simple for you to become pregnant with increasing the eggs developed and introducing the sperm.

"Do you mean like IVF (in vitro fertilization)?"

Yes. If you do choose fertility assistance. This way you are pregnant on the cycle following this coming one.

"I could be pregnant at the end of this coming March?"

Yes

She chose in vitro fertilization and became pregnant in March with a healthy boy. Her son is now two years old.

I am on an appointment over the phone with Julia.

Julia has this question:

"You know we have had a child with mild Asperger's Syndrome. I am pregnant again and I just want to know if this baby is healthy."

Yes, this is a very healthy child that you carry.

"Was my first son's Asperger's in some way related to immunization shots?"

Yes. However not the entire cause.

"Should my second child be immunized? Will he or she get Autism?"

It is not for us to tell you what you should do. It is a feeling within you and you will choose not to immunize until this second baby is older. This is wise to wait until the child is older. One immunization at a time, not several is good. You will have pressure from family and society. This child will not be adversely affected by immunization. Each body responds in its own unique way, as each one has a unique condition.

Carol came in for a reading and after a short time it was very apparent that she also needed a healing, so we did a little of both. She had not been able to get pregnant. It was quite clear in the reading that she had an abortion at some time long ago.

Hello, Dear One, you are holding extreme guilt in the area of your womb and your second chakra. This regards the baby you have lost many years ago. Would you like to talk with us about this?

"I have never told anyone about this! Even my husband does not know. I am so ashamed. I didn't actually lose a baby. I had an abortion when I was fifteen. I have regretted it every day of my life and I beg God to forgive me. I beg this child to forgive me for robbing it of life."

We see that you did have an abortion. You were rather forced to this decision by the boy and parents of the boy. Yes?

"I am terrified I will go to hell for what I have done."

You have punished Self over this for more than twenty years. More than God would think to punish you. There are results or outcomes both in the moment and in the future for all decisions that you make.

"But I took a life!"

You made the decision not to host a life, this is true. You cannot kill a Soul. This Soul lives and has been born to the Earth through another host. You have envisioned yourself as God the Creator if you think you can end the life of a Soul.

What has been done is done. Decide to face your karma when it comes and move on for now. It is for your Creator to judge. Not even you can judge you on this. You can evaluate that you would make a different decision in future circumstance, and thereby learn from your experience. All the punishing of Self for this many years has accomplished nothing. You have severely abused yourself, and you too, are a child of God. We are not happy that you continue to beat up on Self verbally and emotionally. You have been crueler to yourself (a child of God) than you would ever dream to treat another. Always you must forgive yourself, even as you try to do better in the future.

What Spirit is saying in the previous conversation with Carol, is that she made a choice and will face the karma of it in the future. But in the meantime should not continue to harangue herself for the past. Karma can be seen as a balancing of energy rather than a punishment. What you put out comes back to you, positive and negative. In this case she has been creating Hell on Earth for herself by never allowing room for self-forgiveness.

Britt is here in my office and struggling with many decisions. She has been having trouble sleeping and making decisions. She said she can't even decide simple things anymore because she is second-guessing her every thought. She is feeling crippled, as she puts it, and feels close to a breakdown.

CHILDREN AND PARENTING

Britt asks:

"I really hope you can help me. I am thinking about divorcing my husband. Is this a good idea?

You have already filed for divorce we see. In this particular case, yes, it is the path you will take.

"Will my children be okay with the divorce?"

Seldom are the children in favor of divorce. This is happening in their lives, and so the question is not should you divorce but rather, how can you help them the best? What is best for the children in this situation?

These young girls do well with a counselor just for children. One that they can share with. Without feeling they must censor their feelings, they are needing to vent and be heard. There is a bit of broken heart in them for the loss of Dad. Even though they will see him, their hearts break, do you see?

Also they will accept the man you are seeing to be the new husband. They want the love of men very much and are both eager to please. Their own dad has traveled a lot and they have wanted more of him. Now they think they will have less of him, but he is a better dad to them after the divorce because he tries harder. Soon they will soak up the love and affection of an additional dad. See?

"So you do know that I have been dating someone, and do you think he will marry me?"

Yes, You are sure of this as well, or you would not be divorcing. This is truth for you. You would not allow your decision to leave you alone. You looked for a replacement to your husband before you divorced him. Be honest with yourself and you will feel better.

Some of us know from the time we are young that we want to be mothers or fathers someday. That is not true for everyone. It is such a personal decision and sometimes our desires change over time.

This is Trudy:

"I always thought I did not want children. Lately I really do want children. I think about it all the time. I was so sure at one time about not wanting children that I considered getting my tubes tied. Because my own mother was so awful to me, I never trusted my ability to have a good experience. Now I have like such a craving, I can't even explain how huge it is now. Can you please explain this to me?"

You did not want children in your early years and even through your thirties because you were healing. You married a man that did not want children. You traveled the world and built a remarkable career.

You are not the person you once were. You have healed much on many levels. Now you are craving motherhood, also because you have the right partner. One whom you can trust to support you financially and emotionally and in all ways. You know this one will be a good father. You also know that you will be a good mother.

Before there was only fear in you that you would hate being a mother and even hate the child, as you believe your mother hated you. It is true that your mother spent much of her life believing that having a baby ruined things for her. She did not even realize she loved you until she was dying. Then you became very close.

You have grown so much through having a vacant mom that did not want to be a mother. Then you grew even more as you became needed to mother your mother. When you mothered her at the end of her life all of that changed.

Irish Blessing for Children

Lucky stars above you,
Sunshine on your way,
Many friends to love you,
Joy in work and play-
Laughter to outweigh each care,
In your heart a song-
And gladness waiting everywhere
All your whole life long!

CHILDREN AND PARENTING

SEVEN

BUSINESS INTUITION=PROFITS SQUARED

Are you meant to work for others or are you destined to be self-employed? Are you in the right field for you or is there a better choice? What should you do when you come to a fork in the road? Which road is the road to riches? Are you fulfilling your life's purpose? Which job will allow the most growth and happiness? What if you find yourself without a job?

Our work is tied to our income and prosperity, but also to a sense of purpose and value about ourselves. To some it is their entire identity of themselves. We all want to be happy at work and valued. Some are creative and right brained, while many are left brained and prefer things in a linear order. Either way, most of us have a job to do and want that job to fulfill us. We are all motivated by different needs, and then there is money which comes in rather handy too!

In what ways does your job fulfill you? In what ways would you like your job to feel fulfilling? The answers are different for each individual and may also be different at different stages of life. A young stay-home mother is not focused perhaps on what income she generates and a retired person might not be working for money. They both still need to feel fulfilled, useful, and rewarded in some way that they are valued for, or gives them pleasure. Some call it work and others call it hobbies, but we all want our days to amount to a purpose.

People often ask if they are fulfilling their purpose in this life with the work they are doing. Keep in mind that from Spirit's viewpoint your job or the work you do is not always the way in which you fulfill your purpose in life. It is not the work you do in life, but the way you do that work that matters most. It is who you are in the world every day that is the most important part you play.

One woman was told that she was on this planet just to make people feel good about themselves everywhere she went. She was reminded of all the times she struck up a conversation because someone looked lonely. She had compliments for everyone, always seeing the good in others. She showed tolerance, patience, and honesty with everyone. She was not always feeling great or happy herself, but she had the habit of smiling, and sharing her smile with everyone.

It is not the work you do in life, but the way you do that work, that matters most. It is who you are in the world every day that is the most important part you play.

She was a great inspiration to me personally because I knew of the many ailments and pains she dealt with on a daily basis. Her life was often challenging and she suffered with bouts of depression. Her calling was to bring joy to others and she does bring joy, even when she is not feeling joyful.

I have been blessed with Spiritual guidance in my profession all along the way and I am very grateful. In the early 90s when I was busy doing my office work as an accountant I heard Spirit speak inside of my head saying:

Get the phone number '800-KNOWING'

I thought what a great idea for a phone number! I immediately picked up the phone and dialed the number, which turned out to be disconnected. That was good news for me because that meant it was available!

I contacted the phone company to request the phone number asking for it by its digits 800-566-9464. He was very suspicious, it seemed, as he wanted to know how I planned to use the number and why that specific number. He then asked how I knew that the number had just been released that morning!

It was common to sell 800 numbers for more money if they had a useful meaning. I paid no premium and the phone number was transferred to me that same day. So the phone number 800-KNOW-ING was a gift from Spirit and has helped people remember how to find me for over two decades.

Joe has been full of ideas and gung ho about his software development product for years. He knows it is close to being completed and believes in the product, but money is running out and he has had a lot of health issues that have prevented him from working. He is all consumed with the what-ifs and these thoughts are haunting him every day and through the night. He has layers of worry about what if this or that bad thing happens next. He is literally looking for problems and has lost the focus on his goal.

Joe says:

"I am so tired. I am having trouble sleeping too."

You have been through a lot lately. You are resetting your energy, like when a computer or television is buffering. When buffering is going on it cannot be pushed. You just have to be patient.

The body is like unto a battery. It does become exhausted and needs a rest to regain its strength. Sunshine, sleep, living foods such as vegetables and fruits are needed for recharging your body battery. Connecting to Spirit is a way of plugging your body battery into a recharging station. You resist sleep because you have much to do, but it is good for you to get a lot of sleep right now. This is not a good time to keep pushing yourself. Be gentle with yourself much like you might a small child that has been ill or experienced a trauma.

For you, dear one, you are doing really great in some ways and letting yourself down in others. The big picture is to get a program designed that you can make money on over and over again with only small fixes over the next years. The tweaks will become less and less, but you will do an annual update to keep it fresh and to keep reselling. You want to make it a foundation for you to sell again and again. Just like a fine home can give you years of protection with a fresh coat of paint. This product is going to keep on giving, as with beautiful music that you enjoy hearing over and over again. So remember that you keep your mind on the big score, not the individual lines of the music. We realize you must think some of other things. Keep your eye on the big picture and all the other details will get done. You do better in your business when you can say, "I trust the day-to-day will

*work itself out. I am reaching for the big picture." You are caus-
ing a big stress to Self worrying about all that might go wrong
and you are suffering for what may never happen.*

*You have a lovely garden, and when you prepare the soil and
have all of the accoutrements set you are pleased. Then you do not
worry every day if everything will grow, because you know you
have planted the right thing and you must just wait. What are
you doing while you wait? You are having faith that a power
greater than you is at work and you don't worry every minute
if the seedling is doing the job of growing. Keep going on the
big picture. These little tasks are taking some of your attention,
but worse, the constant thinking is taking your energy. Your
energy is in this product and it must be positive, rather than
negative as with worry. Where your (thoughts) energy goes also
goes or comes your money. You are worrying constantly about not
having enough money, and it is leaking from you very fast. Let's
get you back to a deeper daily meditation, for big picture stuff.
You have not been feeling well and you have taken Self out of the
habits that replenish the body battery. Do not waste any time to
say "Oops I shouldn't have let my meditation lapse." No place for
that. There is only room for you to embrace the Now. The Now
is, "I will get back to meditation." The meditation can help you
recharge the body battery and empower the big picture.*

*When you get good sleep you are able to sleep six hours and be
fine. You have a body that repairs itself quite quickly, when it is
well and balanced. What will increase your ability to sleep less
and be more focused, as well as more productive, is meditation.
Meditation will repair the body three times faster than sleep. A
half hour deep meditation equals one and a half hours of sleep.*

A client whose name is Lars had never considered meditation before and was already extraordinarily successful in his field of work. His wife sent him over because his blood pressure was out of control, and he didn't want to take medication.

Lars said:

"So what have you got for me?"

The CEO and executives such as you that are so busy in the head, need deep silence more than anyone. You cannot fathom this at first, because it would not be "doing" something. You like to be doing something. You cannot yet quiet the mind and cannot justify the time to meditate. This for you is why we recommend a walking meditation. Walk alone while you count the breath in, taking twelve counts to inhale, and hold breath for twelve counts. The exhale will be slowly taking twelve counts as well, holding in between the inhale and exhale also twelve counts. It is a walking meditation, so you want to keep the mind still and only focus upon the breath. If you have a mantra or affirmation you can use this in the three equal parts instead of the twelve beats. For you it can perhaps be, "My blood pressure is lower and more relaxed with every breath I take." See? As you breathe in you are saying, "My blood pressure is lower and more relaxed with every breath I take." Then you are holding the breath as you say, "My blood pressure is lower and more relaxed with every breath I take." Then as you exhale you are repeating the affirmation in the same rhythm, "My blood pressure is lower and more relaxed with every breath I take." You are of a nature that cannot be still as yet. You are a person needing constant motion. This is why we are advocating this style of meditation with affirmation. Ultimately we would like you to be able to take this affirmation to a still meditation. There is research to show that certain music can lower blood pressure too. If it pleases you to meditate to soothing music, this is okay for now.

Eventually, all of your five senses need to be able to shut down. This so you are not outside of yourself but rather within. The eyes are closed and you are not focusing on sights, sounds, or movement.

During your half hour walking meditation, as you are walking, you may observe that you have forgotten you are doing a walking meditation. You may forget you were breathing in this way and that you were saying your affirmative mantra. Just come back to it when you remember. Because of your executive type brain you have been very successful. You are constantly wanting to solve this puzzle and that business thought. You are afraid to stop solving. Now the affirmation while walking is so you can say to yourself, even when I am walking I am getting stuff done.

You need a minimum of half an hour of walking every day. This gives you a time to affirm your intentions and what we find with you executives or A types, is that it allows you to justify the time for a walk when there is some merit for working.

Eventually we would like to bring you back to just sitting, eyes closed, and listening only to your heartbeat. Not listening to external sounds. So that is the second phase of your meditation, when you can bring it indoors and be quiet twenty to thirty minutes. If you have to walk ten minutes and say your affirmation before you can be still, that is okay for now. Ultimately with the power of meditation comes a mindfulness and a laser focus on the big goal. We will be teaching you. You are very intuitive, but you have always called it good instincts or a gut feeling. With meditation you will be able to accomplish even more.

I'd like to share a personal story here. My husband was employed for ten years at the same company and was happy with his coworkers and the company. The thing is the company downsized, in a big way, and he was laid off. We had been married a little over a year. I had recently cut my hours as an intuitive consultant, because we had a baby boy and two grade school children for me to take care of.

Did we panic and sweat? Keep in mind that we were well grounded in our faith. We were both active with our meditation practice, and remember, I was intuitive. Did we panic? You're darn right we panicked!! Okay, I will admit I panicked the most. Pete just asked for a reading from me.

Pete asked whatever it was he asked (it was eighteen years ago). We both remember what Spirit said to us:

> *Your company is not your source of income. God is your source. The Universe provides through people and circumstances, but they are not your source or your provider. You have given this job loyalty and thought that they would give you job security and safety.*
>
> *You have been aware of some opportunities that could be good for you in other companies. You stayed with your job you think for loyalty, but really for fear of change. You feared risk of accelerating your career would equal lack of security. You have fear of change, but you see change will happen anyway. If you risk nothing...you risk even more. There are not any promises that you can prevent change. You were loyal to the company, but there was no loyalty in return. Better to be loyal to your personal adventure and embrace change. Do not worry, Dear One, you will be blessed in many ways. Nothing is your true source but God.*

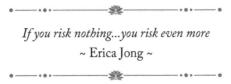

If you risk nothing...you risk even more
~ Erica Jong ~

This reminded me of something I once read in a course I led on prosperity several years earlier. The book that I wanted was still on the bookshelf. It is a book by John Randolph Price called *The Abundance Book*. A small green book that takes very little time to read but makes a big impact on us every time we read it. We started the forty-day prosperity plan that is laid out in the book.

One of the affirmations in The Abundance Book goes like this. "Money is not my supply. No person, place or condition is my supply. My awareness, and understanding and knowledge of the all-providing activity of the Divine Mind within me is my supply.

What happened to us after Pete was unemployed for several months? Well, Pete got a couple of consulting jobs while he was looking for a new permanent job. He made more per hour and worked less hours. He worked from home too. All said and done, when we filed our taxes for that year, our family income was within a few dollars of the income for the previous year!

In hindsight we saw some great benefits that came from his being laid off. He was home to enjoy our son's first steps and early walking. We had more time as a family to hike, bike, swim, and play. After a few months, one of the consulting jobs hired him with an increase in his previous salary. This brought us to San Diego, which we call home today. There are many good memories here that would never have been made if we didn't make the move for Pete's new job.

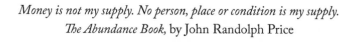

Money is not my supply. No person, place or condition is my supply.
The Abundance Book, by John Randolph Price

I met Rex at a party. He was introduced to me by the hostess, who told me he was the most successful realtor in her company. He came to see me and admitted being out of his comfort zone. He told me that he sure never thought he would ever go to see "anyone like me."

I said, "Why, because I'm too old for you?"

He laughed good-naturedly, and I laughed with him. He was clearly at least twenty-five years my senior.

He relaxed some and began with his questions

"I think this might sound a little foolish, but I want to quit a perfectly good career. I want to be a life coach and help people. I know there are a lot of life coaches out there, but I just know this is right for me. I feel it deep within me that this is my calling. Can I do this, and make enough money as a life coach?

> *When you have a passion for something, the Universe has this same passion for you. You have been very successful as a real estate agent. You have been redirected in your heart and you no longer want to be in real estate.*
>
> *To be a coach and for this to be a pleasing success for you will depend on you first finding an area of expertise that sets you apart from the other coaches. You have a great success in real estate, both residential and business. You have some investments that you have rented out, so this is property management. Choose to be a coach in the area where you are expert and can share what you know, as in real estate. If you wish to coach in other areas over time this will come to you as well.*
>
> *You have already begun a course of learning coaching, yes?*

BUSINESS INTUITION=PROFITS SQUARED

"Yes. I have this huge gut feeling and I just know this is what I want to do. I was kind of afraid you would tell me not to do it."

You have made a good choice and know well how to hire others to train you and do small tasks for you. You have some money to live on and income from rental property. The moment the decision was made within you was the moment that we see it was already fulfilled.

When you have a passion for something, the Universe has this same passion for you. All the Universe will bring forth an army of energy and wisdom that will stack up behind your intention and literally make the pieces fall into place for you.

You are then turning all the little pieces over to your higher mind, higher consciousness, Holy Spirit, depending on what you want to call it. It does work for you to set your goal and focus on just this outcome of being a sought after coach. All of the universe will bring forth an army of energy and wisdom that will stack up behind your intention and literally make the pieces fall into place for you.

You do need to begin writing down all the steps that contributed to your success in real estate. You have forgotten many little things. Pick apart your success and put it down in writing so that you have a workbook of sorts. It will bring you quicker success to have a book and or workbook.

Jim doesn't share with a lot of people that he meditates. He began a couple of months ago when his doctor recommended meditation to reduce his stress and blood pressure. He has asked Divine for additional advice on how he can reduce his habit of high stress.

So in theory because you are the executive of this, your job is only to create the big intentions. The growth of company and profits. If you can develop single-minded intention, you will create and attract the right people to carry all of it out for you. You are as the maestro of the orchestra, whose job is not to make any of the music but only to decide its tempo as it reveals itself. Keep your eye on North Star, you end up North. Keep your eye on the ultimate goal, and do not let anything else penetrate the mind. Especially do not allow doubt.

Karen is successful in business but wants more. She is not feeling satisfied with her level of intuition or her meditation. After expressing her frustration to Spirit this was the reply.

Keep to your meditation consistently, and you are getting closer all the time to the deep connection you are craving. You are growing in your intuition.

Then ultimately you will get to the still mind and the sound of creation beyond those of ocean and birds. This is referred to as Om. We want you to get in touch with your intuition, and you want that too. In order to do this you must be the CEO and manager of your five senses. You need to be able to say to your five senses—turn off for the time I tell you. You oversee your five senses and you purposely get to the power where you can shut them all off. When you get to where you can do this you will be able to see, hear, and touch a higher consciousness. This will allow you to experience your sixth sense.

We will tell you, if you are wondering what on the earth would sixth sense of smell do for me. But even as a business person, you get in touch with the sixth sense and you feel in your mind's eye. Follow with us for a moment, if we are not too far out of your comfort zone. You think, I feel like I smell curry and you begin thinking maybe is dinner cooking somewhere. But you know it is not dinner cooking. Now this interesting smell of curry is coming from nowhere except for your sixth sense of smell. For the purpose of guiding you, Spirit, or you may prefer to think higher Self, uses this to put into your mind a craving. Next thing you know you are saying to your spouse or partner, "Let's go out for Indian food!" So in the evening you are well prepared for an Indian feast. You are then dining at a particular Indian restaurant, at a particular time, and a moment of particular timing. When a particular helpful resource shows up. This is when you meet the CEO of your next company. You meet someone who is the expert you have been looking for to help on your product. You may meet the new best friend who then turns out to be married to the next great partner of your next great adventure in business.

We are telling you that you will not know usually what is the reason for the intuition, just to follow it. In time it will pay out for you. This is to follow intuition and not know where it will lead. It will always lead to amazing results. Even not really knowing what will pay out of it. This is one of those ways the sixth sense of smell and taste can actually be used to guide you in the best intuitive direction.

Shelly told me she thought her grandmother was visiting her from Heaven. She explained the reason she felt this way. She never felt any conversation coming through from the other side, and things in the house didn't move. She could be anywhere and feel a love wash through her that she just knew was Grandmother. This was always accompanied by the smell of her grandmother's perfume. This is a great way for our loved ones to reach out to us. Many people have shared with me that they sometimes notice a certain smell relating to a family member that has passed away. For example, a mother who has passed away may come to watch over you or comfort you, and come through as the smell of her favorite perfume, or a food she was well remembered for cooking.

I have a story related to this. Many years ago I was asked to come to Newport Harbor, to investigate a boat that had just been purchased. I was asked to investigate the boat for haunting as some very strange things had been happening on board.

They told me that it had recently come loose from its mooring to the dock during the night. The boat traveled against the current and was found in the slip of the original owner the following morning!! The original owner of the boat had passed away years earlier.

I never want to know any details about a haunting ahead of time so as to prevent any interference with my intuition. In this case I only knew I was going to investigate a boat and that the new owners thought something strange was going on. I had done investigating such as this before.

On my way driving to the assignment, I smelled the loveliest aroma of tobacco. I don't smoke, but the fresh smell of tobacco was rich spicy, sweet, and an unmistakably delicious earthy smell (it reminded me of how delicious coffee smells when you open a fresh new can). All of the car windows were closed and no air was coming in from the outside. Oh, how intriguing, I thought, my first clue.

As I stepped onto the boat I had many experiences, but only one I want to share with you right now. In one of the rooms, I was enveloped in the same rich smell of tobacco. I was then told that this was the main salon. Later I found that this was in fact the sleeping and private living area for John Wayne and this was his boat "The Wild Goose!"

Some business persons can literally smell money when they are onto the right idea of something that is a money-making idea. A form or way of intuitive smell that says *yes* for their ideas. Saying, "You've got it. This is a money-making idea."

Connie developed an insatiable hunger for Spiritual knowledge when her sister passed away last year. She has told me that all the books and material she reads feel like Truth and yet she keeps being concerned that in some way she might be violating her religion.

"I want to develop intuition and also be able to manifest the things I want. I'm Christian and I don't want to change my religion. How can I be intuitive and honor my religion?"

Meditation can also be described as the listening side of prayer. When you say your prayers from deep in your heart, you have noticed a difference in the connectedness you feel to God. Yes?

"Yes, I do feel that."

After you connect in prayer in this way, simply stop the thinking, while holding that special connection you feel in your heart. Listen to the silence inside of you as you feel the splendid Grace of God.

We are saying all of this because without the practice of meditation you cannot make a complete connection. On your computer you might say I have no internet connection, so I cannot look up that information. Think of meditation as your connection to Spirit. Mediation does not have to be a religious practice. It is a focus practice which allows you a complete connection. It is a practice of turning inward to go above and beyond the five senses of the physical earth, and spend time with Creator. The mysteries of the universe are where the money-making ideas and wisdom are above and beyond anything you see as real with the physical eye. The five senses are merely a distraction keeping you more earthbound.

"I want to know something before everyone else. I want to be ahead of the brightest thinkers in my company."

You will tell us you want to be better than the competition. You will have the edge when you can understand your intuition and sixth sense. First you must return to meditation. You already know that you are welcoming meditation and that you have missed it. So you don't have to get comfortable with the idea, but you do need a deeper habit. As you develop your habit of meditation the ideas will come.

We find the ones that excel best in intuition keep an intuitive journal. You will become more acquainted with your intuition by keeping track of each message and serendipity. An example of serendipity might be when you think of your friend Christopher and you are all of the sudden seeing a bumper sticker that is saying Christopher. A serendipity is a sign that you are in sync with the Universe.

So in this example, it would be a verification that yes, you do need to contact Christopher. With the writing down of all intuition, serendipity, and all confirmations of it, you will increase the value you put on it, and this gives to you a wonderful power. This is a way of affirming that you know this intuitive stuff has value. What you place value (focus) on will increase.

You would not think to study Spanish, or another language, without seeing what the words look like. The language of intuition by its very nature is intangible. So to make it more tangible, and to learn this new language, it does become important to write it down.

Just by your saying "I intend to increase my intuition," it will be done. Then you put the power of tools behind it and it accelerates. Also this will help you to gain confidence and verification of your intuition.

So you are going to begin this intuitive journal, and it can include anything you want to say in it. Honor the accuracy you experience. Do not discount that which does not seem to have accuracy yet. The information may turn out to be mind chatter, but could also be accurate to you, as you obtain the whole picture over time. You will only know if you have recorded that which you believe is intuition.

Many years ago I could not figure out how to survive financially, physically, or emotionally with two children and no help on the horizon. Many sleepless nights I worried that we would be homeless in Denver. We had just moved to Denver and didn't know a soul. Things looked very bleak at this time. I prayed for God to please help me and tell me what to do next to fix everything.

Hello Dear One.

You need time when you are not trying to solve anything. It ties into why you are craving sleep. When you are asleep you are in surrender of the conscious mind. You are giving it over and letting your thinking be at peace during sleep. You are needing to quit trying to solve all of this from an intellectual perspective. It is only really that you need to release it and let it be solved. So you are thinking how you are going to orchestrate the whole thing yourself and you are overwhelmed.

It would be similar, we would say, if you try to go to the airport and figure out how to get from LAX to NY La Guardia without a guide. You would not be able to figure out which gate, which plane, or which transfers without some sort of a guidance system. But you do not need to design the system, you can just follow the system that is in place and you will arrive. But if you listen and follow signs, even within what looks like chaos all around, you will find yourself guided to the right gate and the right plane which takes you to connections, allowing you to get to your destination.

Just like at a busy airport, your destination is known, but you don't know how to get there. It is the same in business going forward. You know where you are destined to go, but you don't know yet how to get there. You must learn to follow the signs of intuition. But because of human nature you want to figure out and you want to orchestrate it and take control. You can do the parts that need your action. But to figure out the details of what will go where and how in the world you will get there is not possible right now. There are things at this time you cannot figure out yet. This is time to use faith and still doing your job but your job is not to spend a lot of time to go over and over with worries. This is not taking you where you need to go. The mind

BUSINESS INTUITION=PROFITS SQUARED

is constantly tumbling with thoughts going around and around the issues and worries.

So it is a time when meditation can help you. Even just time where you are quiet and say everything is already okay. Six months from now it is all worked out and you are going to just know that. Do you see?

If you want the sun to come up, you can think of ways all night long if you want to, but it will still come up when it comes up; it is not in your hands. This too, is not in your hands.

Trying to figure this out is similar to digging up the garden when it is trying to grow. Of course this doesn't really help, and in fact much the opposite.

Nate is a college student. He has already told me he feels burnt out with school. He thinks he may have chosen the wrong thing to study and still has no idea what he should pursue for work.

Nate says:

"I think I have totally been studying the wrong thing for three years. Do I have a calling or purpose that I am supposed to be following? I chose engineering in school and I'm about two and a half, almost three years in. I do okay, but I don't love it and I don't know if I should finish."

Yes, it is important to finish. You will use the education more than you know at this time. Your real love here seems to be music. You are not so much the most amazing musician when it comes to performing. What you have as a special talent is the love of music, and the judgment of the sounds. You are good with the words, but even more with the beat and the feeling of music.

Like being an engineer with math and taking it musical. You are making music out of the equations.

Because of the engineering and the employment you take, this brings you to the right situation. You are more creative like an inventor. The knowledge and skill will come together with opportunity and then you will know your calling.

Shari has five grown children and one grandchild. She is facing divorce. She has to go to work or do something to earn a living.

Shari asks:

"I am so scared and I have no idea what I can possibly do for work that will make any money for me. I'm not even good at anything except raising kids. I never got much in the way of education, and what I do have is outdated. Can you tell me what I should be doing?"

Hello, Dear One. You are everyone else's confidant and you are a good listener. You are not so good at sharing your own feelings, and you are feeling very lonely. Your self-esteem is low. It is time to ask others what you are good at. They see a lot of value in you that you do not see.

We will tell you about work. You are very artistic and this is really all you have ever enjoyed to do. You buy things a lot. We see that you never leave them as they are. You are liking to paint furniture and use the glue gun to attach this and that. You are quirky in your view of things and there is a lot of money in the unusual. This is why everyone tells you they love the things that you create. You are adept at sewing when you want to create what you can't find or embellish something. You

BUSINESS INTUITION=PROFITS SQUARED

are the one to shop the junk and make it a piece of art. Your friends have told you that you could sell these things, but you do not really believe them?

"I guess not, or maybe I wish that it was true. I wouldn't know where to begin doing a business like this."

First there is going to be some education possibilities and some money in support coming to you for spouse support. You do not need to make a full income to support yourself. Most of what you need is to make an income that makes you feel worthy and fulfilled. You are needing work as an expression of who you are. It becomes your new identity, because being a mother is not enough focus for you anymore. When you feel good you are a wonderful gift to the world in your listening, counseling, and beautifying of the place. What a wonderful purpose in life to make others feel good and enjoy the art you create.

We would recommend that you get some education in interior design and also in business finance. This more to give you confidence in yourself. You are needing to get a better sense of the value of you, and the value of the things you create.

Begin to shop the high-end stores. Travel a bit to places that are tourist locations, and become familiar with the very unique places to shop. In this you will gather knowledge, and ideas will accumulate in you.

We would like for you to collect business cards or contact information from each shop. Although there is not something you will use them for just yet. In time, you will be able to hire another woman in need of a job and this will make you both happy. You bring the junk and the ideas and she will execute the plan as you have hired her to do.

BUSINESS INTUITION=PROFITS SQUARED

The main reason for the education will be so that you feel worthy and equal to some of the people to whom you will be selling your creations. The creations are very good, but your self-esteem is not so good. There are many classes and adventures coming to you that will help you with this.

You do not need to change the world with what you do in this life. You only need to be who you are and that changes Everything!

BUSINESS INTUITION=PROFITS SQUARED

EIGHT
INTUITION WITH PETS

Dog's are man's best friend and so are cats and other furry friends. Numerous people on the planet benefit from the love and joy pets bring into their lives. We have two little furry friends in our home. They greet us each time we come home as if they haven't seen us in months. They flip, turn, jump, bark, make a huge fuss and leave no doubt that they love us. Blizzard looks like his name because he is all white. He has never been robust and healthy, he loves the outdoors, and has the most adorable sound he makes in conversation. We have another dog named TuTu and she is actually Blizzard's daughter. She is a full-figured girl and bosses him around. She is always getting feisty and rousing up some play. She races him to the door for walks and prevents him from getting up the stairs before her at bedtime. They both love to cuddle and they sleep the night in our bed. They also bring us joy twice a day when they take us for walks. We love our beautiful community, enjoy walking the trails, and look forward to our sunset views. We know we would not take as many walks if not for our dogs, and we are very grateful they get us out. So many times when we have thought we were feeling too tired and lazy to walk it has been just the blessing we needed.

Cats bring great joy, comfort, and peace to the homes they run too. For many pet owners they are the perfect pet. When we first married we had three cats. I love cats too, but now that they have passed away we will not be a cat family, only because we have since found my husband is highly allergic to kitty cats.

People often ask questions about their pet's health and behavioral issues.

Jacki is an adorable Bichon whom I have known since he was a baby. His owner recently called me because he was whining constantly and nothing seemed to comfort him. He was refusing dog food and wasn't being his spunky self so his owner asked,

"What can I do for Jacki?"

Hello, Dear One. There is a lot of pain in his mouth. This little love of yours has a bad tooth infection. It is causing even him to feel sick in the tummy. He will not eat because it hurts, but also the tummy is not welcoming food.

"He had a teeth cleaning fairly recently, under anesthesia"

He will need to be seen again soon.

Jacki went to have his teeth checked. He needed two teeth pulled and received antibiotics. Jacki is a very vocal dog, but due to the language barrier, it was difficult to explain to his best friend where it was hurting.

Lucas is a really sweet baby Lab who has just been adopted by a family of four. The youngest child in the family was terrified of all

dogs, and the hope was to help him learn to enjoy a family dog and get rid of his fear. Everyone loved Lucas and, nevertheless, it slowly became the mom alone who fed and cared for the dog. The father grew up with pets belonging only outside and was not about to change his thinking. They lived in Southern California and the dog had a warm and cozy doghouse. The mom loved to hike the hills near home and took Lucas with her every day.

When Mom had an injury to her back in a car accident and needed surgery, the routine with Lucas changed dramatically. Lucas was stuck in the yard all day alone. He ate the hose, the fence, the plants, and dug holes in the yard for entertainment.

The youngest child still didn't feel inclined to interact with the dog very much and the oldest was committed to sports seven days a week with little playtime. Dad was not used to doing his job and all the jobs Mom used to do as well. Poor Lucas was lonely and sad. This was the advice Spirit gave.

Lucas is a companion to Marie, his mom. He will feel complete if he can just lie beside her and share his love. Marie will heal many times faster with Lucas's love and she will even get back to full activity soon. Now that Lucas is potty trained it would be helpful to both of them if he can be in the house where he will try to help. He is still very young and does need toys provided for him to destroy.

The youngest child is to be assigned to walk Lucas on a leash. We prefer he would take obedience class with Lucas. He does not mind Lucas, but has not bonded with the dog. When your young boy has responsibility for Lucas, he begins to bond, and love him. Lucas will be a very loyal and loving member of your family. Shame to give up on Lucas; this is a partnership that will be very rewarding to all. Do what we have said for three months before you give up on Lucas.

Dogs as service animals have been around for a long time. They have helped many blind and disabled people to live life more fully and enabled them to get around on their own. We now have in-service dogs that help people with issues of high anxiety, trauma, abuse, as well as heart conditions and more. These little blessings have been of service to many people who would otherwise be quietly suffering alone at home, isolated from the world. Most dogs are happiest when they have a purpose. This is the question of one of my clients.

"Do you think a service dog would help me?"

Yes, Dear One, a dog or a cat would be very helpful for you. You are allergic to many animals of fur. Choose carefully an animal that you are not allergic to and of a size and temperament that you can manage. You are very lonely and this is the main reason you are needing someone to belong with, someone to talk to. Also the anxiety you experience, though it does not go away, it is greatly improved, as you will travel to the market with your new companion. This dog, as we see you choose a dog, is about two and a half years old. It is best for you to have a female. She is very dull in nature compared to what others are looking for. You do not want the most eager one but rather the quieter and more reluctant one. She has anxiety too, but together you create calm for one another. She has already been named; please let her keep the name.

I was surrounded by pets and lots of animals growing up. The family dog that I grew up with was named Teddy. She was the one I talked things over with when life seemed unfair and when I needed to cry on someone's shoulder. She was a great friend and lived until we were both sixteen. When you lose a pet, you lose a member of the family. For us this happened just months after my dad became paralyzed and I cried so very hard. The entire family felt such a deep loss and we all seemed to drag ourselves through the days.

I wondered, so I asked God if I would see Teddy in heaven. God told me yes and that gave me a lot of peace.

We also had many cats, two parakeets, and numerous fish from carnivals. Tadpoles captured at the park were set free in our back yard pond. We raised five Rhode Island Red chickens. My brother even had a small black snake with a red ring around its neck. I loved my cat Puff more than anything and I secretly felt that I was her favorite too. My dad believed strictly in outdoor pets, but sometimes I was allowed to have Puff sleep with me. She was a beautiful butterscotch color with fur as long and fluffy as a bunny. We also had a huge, pure white bunny with red eyes that Grandma and Grandpa had given us. I loved to get in the bunny cage with Whitey the bunny and just be with him. My favorite time to sit in the cage was when it was raining outside, because we were kept dry by the roof even though the rain was pouring down all around us and pounding on the roof.

My grandparents had a dog named Lucky who was big enough to ride when we were little. They also raised rabbits and canaries. My other grandparents had a midsized black dog that grandpa treated like a person.

Ginger was the first dog of my own that I received for my thirtieth birthday before I had children. She was a beautiful petite Visla with hair the color of a stick of cinnamon. As a baby her eyes were emerald green. She was my first baby and I took her everywhere. When Ginger was just three months old I went hiking in the woods with her. It was a warm day, but there were still patches of snow on the ground and the river was rushing with newly melted snow. When she fell off a log into the river, I dove into the melted ice right behind her without hesitation. I often hiked four to six hours a day and once she was fully grown she not only kept up with me, she would run at top speed way out ahead and come back so that she ran at least three to four times the hike that I did. She was a running and hunting breed and she could run for hours without pause.

When I was thirty-four, I had to give her up for her own best good. It was a heart-wrenching experience. I had a baby and a two year old. I was getting a divorce and would be moving to an apartment with no place for her to run. Spirit gave me this advice.

You need to take care of your children and will not be able to do both. You are in stress to the point something has to give. You cannot care for her and give her what she needs to fully thrive. She loves you and always will, she will not forget you, but she will get over you. She will be well loved and lead a contented and healthy life. Do not pity her, she will be able to have a better life and it is better for you.

The family that adopted her was a gift from heaven for us. The mom was a stay-home mom who took long hikes every day. Ginger would have two school age, dog-loving boys to play with. This family owned a large ranch which was used as an animal rescue, but Ginger would be their house dog.

Clark Kent was a rescue dog and the best dog they ever had, his owner told me. Even though Clark's parents got divorced they both shared visitation times with Clark. Clark Kent traveled back and forth between houses with the kids. This is what Clark's owner asked on his behalf.

"Clark is fifteen now and usually he still acts like a puppy. Something has changed recently and he just isn't the same. Should I take him to the vet? I am so worried and I don't know how I would explain this change to the vet. It's subtle and maybe he is just depressed, but I feel like it's more than that. I hope he is all right. I don't know how I would live without him. Our son is leaving for college and Clark will be devastated. Is Clark going to be leaving us soon?"

Clark Kent will be staying with you and very much alive. He did have a stroke it seems. He is not the same exactly. Mostly just a slower boy. He is also not seeing so very well and there is a need for moving slow when one cannot see. Yes? He has never mentioned it, however, he does hurt more and this is why he does not get on the bed anymore. He would love you to lift him up to the bed more and the sofa too. It is a good time for a check-up at the vet and there is something to soften his hurting found there. He does mention the chicken you used to cook for him. He would like some of that.

"That is so funny, I was on this diet where I made chicken every day for breakfast and I was sharing it with him. I quit the diet last week. I guess he liked our breakfast together.

"I am relieved that he is okay. I still want to know if I will have to make a decision for him at some point soon. I know he is getting older and I worry how I will know when it is time."

No. You won't be deciding that. When it is time there is no decision for you but to love him. This you can do.

Here is another example of the depth of devotion a loving pet and owner can share. Sweet Melissa was rather like a lab and golden mix. She had been the sidekick of George for sixteen years. Melissa went everywhere George did. They backpacked and she had her own pack to carry her own food. They went to the store and she waited in the truck. He went to work and she lay there all day content to watch him work as a landscape architect inside or outside. She tolerated and shared George with the occasional girlfriend. When George mountain biked she ran along and kept up. Now she was not feeling well. George asks this question.

"We have been to the vet and I know Melissa is dying. She won't eat and doesn't even move all day. I carry her out to go to the bathroom before bed, and yesterday she just lay there in the grass. I know she is tired and needs to let go. I won't put her down, I just won't. What can I do to make her more comfortable?"

Dear One, Melissa knows her place as your guardian and your best friend. She does not want to leave you all alone. She believes that you will not be okay without her. Who will take care of you and look after you? She knows you are suffering and sad. She has determined not to leave you.

Speak to your sweet Melissa. Convince her that you will be okay. She looks to you, and she will not surrender without your blessing. You will see her in Spirit one day.

INTUITION WITH PETS

After this reading George and I were both in tears. George had a heart to heart with Melissa and when she left this world, she was embraced in his arms.

Calvin is large for a cat and has the thickest fur I have ever felt on a feline. He is proud and smart and feisty too. When Calvin's owner, Mark, put cat treats into the cabinet above the fridge, Calvin scaled the counters to the top of the refrigerator and somehow climbed inside the cabinet. He freed the can of cat treats and ate the whole thing! Mark tried, and tried, to train Calvin to be an indoor cat. Calvin would have none of it. Calvin could be nowhere in sight, but when his owner opened the door—*whoosh*—and a streak of fur would fly by to the great outdoors and take off.

Mark asked:

"What can I do about Calvin? We live near an open canyon and there are a lot of coyotes and I am afraid he will not live long if he is outside. He loves his outdoor adventures so much though, and he outsmarts us constantly to get out. We have tried squirting him with a water gun to keep him off the table and he turns it into a game. Squirting him when he tries to get outside is just as futile for us and fun for him. Now my wife is pregnant and the other night she was out running after Calvin. Can you help explain to Calvin that he will get killed out there?"

Dear One, your Calvin is yours to take care of, this is true, but not yours to hold captive. He does not want to live inside of a house. He is not a house cat. He wants to live a life of adventure and the coyotes are half the fun. He says "Don't worry I can outrun them. I like to travel a lot of places. No one tells you to stay home because you might have trouble outside. A life indoors is not a life worth living to me."

The owner recently let me know that Calvin lived nine more years as a happy cat coming and going on his own terms.

We love our pets and they love us. We need each other and we all need someone to give our love to as well.

I guess all we can really say is...pets are people too!

INTUITION WITH PETS

189

NINE

KNOWING YOUR INTUITIVE VOICE

L iving a life connected to God and Intuition is living a life connected to joy and peace in Body, Mind, and Spirit. Are you living in peace and joy? Are you happy and balanced in all areas of your life? Is your body healthy, fit, and working for you? Do you feel peaceful and content with everything in your life?

You deserve happy relationships that are fulfilling in a way that you are content with. It is important to feel connection and peace with your religious and spiritual self.

How about your mind? Do you keep active with new learning, thoughts, and pursuits?

We all know what comes next is to examine any areas of weakness, imbalances, or discontentment. If any area of your life is out of balance and bothering you, the first step is recognition. When any part of us or our life is not healthy, we must ask what we are in need of to feel fulfilled and balanced in this area of our life. We must ask what we need to add or increase and make adjustments. It is just as important to ask what must I do away with?

Perhaps there are habits or activities that no longer support the life you choose to live. People, places, and things all have a time and purpose in our lives. Do you hold onto things long after you are over them, or after they have lost usefulness? This includes emotional attachments as well as material things.

If you find yourself unable to release items or relationships that no longer support joy and enhance your life, there is probably some fear there. Ask yourself what you might be holding onto that you no longer need. The reasoning here is often...

"I will keep this just in case I need it in the future."

The thinking behind that kind of reasoning for holding on to things actually goes a little bit deeper. You might be really thinking, "What if I can't afford to replace this?" or "What if no one else comes along to be my friend?" Check your thoughts, and observe if you are clutching too tightly to patterns, people, and things when you know you need to move on.

Letting go of situations, people, and things gives a clear message that you believe in the Universe to provide for you when the time comes. The belief behind giving is, "I will always attract what I need when I need it."

Continue to ask yourself again—What time wasters or bad habits need to be eliminated to create peace in my life? Peace is our goal. God is always cheering for us and desires all of us to have peace and joy in our lives.

Now that you have recognized an area of your life that may need adjusting, let's see how best to accomplish the changes. I love goal setting, because it works. The first step is to have a clear mental goal. The self-analysis I just discussed should help you get more clarity. The next step is the most important and that is to simply write down your goals. It has been proven that those who write out their goals have a far better assurance of achieving them.

KNOWING YOUR INTUITIVE VOICE

A lot of people come for a 'reading' with an idea in their head of what they desire in life, but have never written those desires down. Whether it is love, money, health, or something else it is imperative that you write it down, to achieve the desired result.

You may think you have a clear idea of what you want. I challenge you to write it down on white paper in blue or black ink right now. Use the margin of the book if you like. Take a moment and write a goal down right now.

I wonder how many of you wrote a goal? I never stop and do something an author asks me to, because I don't want to stop reading. However, if you don't do this you really won't get the benefit of a goal that has been brought out of the ether and into form. The point is, when you do write down your goal you will find you have to be more exact. To write down a goal is to make a firm decision on the goal. The difference between deciding and declaring in writing makes all the difference. Once a goal has been decided and declared in this way it is done as far as the universe is concerned. Heaven and Earth unite to match the truth you have just declared.

A goal works best when it is written as if it has already been manifested. For example, you might declare, "I love the way my body looks and feels." Now write down some steps that will be needed to get you to your goal. Things you must do before you can get to the goal that equals your perfect body. Here is an example of some tasks you may need to accomplish your goal:

- Join a gym—thirty minute exercise three times a week
- Establish a walking partner—walk every other day
- Therapist—heal PTSD re: trauma
- Get out gym clothes & try on—purchase gym shoes
- Hire nutritionist - begin eating better—eat healthy live foods

KNOWING YOUR INTUITIVE VOICE

Setting goals is huge for getting clear on what you would like to create. The key that must be in place to bring it all together and manifest your goal is meditation.

Have you ever thought to yourself—maybe I should try meditation?

I hope you will begin a consistent meditation practice. This will support a deeper meditation. The deeper the meditation the quicker and easier it is to manifest your goals. For optimum successes in meditation, these are some bullet points to remember.

1. Create a special space or chair for your meditation.
2. Sit with spine straight, in lotus position, or straight back chair.
3. Meditate at the same time each day.
4. Morning and evening are best times.
5. Close your eyes and turn them upward to gaze upon the location of the third eye. This is a reference to the chakra located in the forehead. The third eye is not a physical eye. It is located in the center of the forehead just above the level of the eyebrows. This is the center that must awaken for intuition.
6. Focus inward on the breath completely. Do not try to control the breath, just observe.
7. Focus upon each nuance of the cool air entering your nostrils, and the warmer air leaving out the mouth.
8. Notice how the body moves with each inhalation and exhalation.

Pay attention to the breath as if you are responsible for watching a toddler near the water's edge and you can't let your mind lose track of this breath for a moment. Meditation is easier said than done but well worth the effort.

The rewards of meditation are beyond measure. Here are just a few proven benefits of meditation:

- deeper sleep
- less sleep required
- normalizing blood pressure
- reduced stress, reduced conflict within relationships
- and much, much, more

Best of all you will get to know yourself, finding release from internal trauma and discord. Even better, you will know for yourself a relationship with Divine and this makes All Things Possible.

If you want to awaken intuition, meditation is a necessity. There are different ways to enhance and understand your intuition, to be sure, but first you must awaken it and meditation is the only way.

The most successful people who wish to awaken spiritually and intuitively develop a routine of practice for their meditation that is consistent. This works best because your body expects to relax into meditation at its regular time and the mind begins to crave it's time to be quiet and be in Spirit. Just as you might look forward to lunch or dinner for the food, perhaps as well as the break from work, you will find yourself craving your meditation time.

If I rush out the door without meditation, my whole day is different. If I go to bed thinking I am just too tired to meditate, my sleep is not as deep and peaceful. Try a meditation routine morning and evening, twenty to thirty minutes each time for thirty days and you will be hooked on the best habit of your life. Your life will change for the better with each passing day.

Maybe you have tried to manifest, and maybe you have heard of the law of abundance or positive thinking. These practices can be easy, or seem very difficult to do. The difference of why one person will have success and another may not, depends on that person being able to reach a state of consciousness or connectedness with Source. To manifest what you dream of and to attract all that you desire, it is first necessary to connect with the Source of everything. Connecting to God is what meditation is all about.

Imagine you wish to call out for pizza (or any food you wish). You dial up the number for the restaurant, but the connection is lost before the pizza parlor answers. Do you think, oh well, I will just speak my order through the phone anyway and hope it arrives? Not if you're hungry, you don't! You would make sure you have dialed the correct number, and have a good connection, because you want that pizza to arrive, and arrive exactly as you want it.

Maybe you place an online order for food delivery. First you have to make sure you have an internet connection and then you must be sure you are connected to the proper website. Type your order in bold if you like, but it will never get though unless you make the proper connection first.

Meditation is like your cell phone or internet connection. Is your connection weak, or strong? Do you have one bar or four? You are the one that must practice in this case to make sure you have a full four bars of connection before you dial up the Big Order Center of the Universe. With repeated practice meditation helps you to achieve full reception and gives you those bars you need to make the connection. Through the regular practice of meditation, you will find more peace, love, and joy in every area of your life. You cannot live a life intuitively in tune without meditation.

Now you have the understanding of how goal setting and meditation are a powerful combination of tools.

I would like to share a couple of readings where clients incorporated goal setting. Our bodies are a complex and Divine creation. Some people just need exercise and eating awareness. Other people have an illness that needs addressing. In any case there will be tasks toward achieving the desired goal.

Kayte came for an intuitive session and had many questions. Finally she asked the one question that was really bothering her.

Kayte asked Divine:

"Do you think it is time for me to have surgery? Will it be successful?"

Yes, it is time for surgery. You have been contemplating this for some time. It is a success and also a big adjustment.

Kayte has been overweight her entire life and felt like an outcast. She did not mention that she was thinking of gastric bypass surgery.

You have a healthy outlook and you love to exercise. You are very fit and also too heavy to keep active and will be breaking down your joints. You will have great success with this surgery. In order to feel okay with it you will need therapeutic counseling. You have avoided dating and, although you have great male friends, you do not like to be touched. You will attract many men and be very sought after. This makes you feel uncomfortable. You must solve this aspect or you will not allow Self to be slim. Also you will need support for the changes as they are greater than you are aware.

"Okay, well should I be doing this on my own without surgery? I feel a little guilty taking the easy way out here. Should I be doing this myself with will power?"

Sorry to say, but you cannot do this alone. Without surgery, you will fail as before. If you have surgery you still will require those who can to help you. This has been a lifelong pattern. See? You must change much in the belief system to sustain this. Also surgery is not easy for you. It is worth it to you though and you will come through healthier than now. More able to tackle the project of being an average size as well as fit.

You are very lacking in pro-biotics in the system. You will need to take these, it appears, for a very long time to support the body system. You were very ill when young. Looks to be three years and also to four years old?

'Yes, I almost died and I have still a tendency to asthma and upper respiratory problems."

Your nutritionist should know this. All is affecting all. You crave food and sugars for fuel and comfort and literally feel sometimes you will collapse without the food. Your brain is controlled by your gut. You have said you feel possessed sometimes that you cannot keep from eating, as if you are being made to do it. Well, in a way this has been true. The body system is not working as a system. Better to have a nutritionist that is a doctor for full understanding of what you need. The balancing will be complex for a length of time.

Janice has come from the doctor who told her that she needs to lose at least twenty-five pounds and get in better shape. She asked Spirit for advice.

"I go to the doctor every year, and every year I weigh more and have the same complaints. My level of energy is nonexistent, to the point that if I work out I have to come home and lie down. I need a nap every day. I try to lose weight and just don't have any will power. I need food or I am so exhausted I just might as well stay in bed. What should I do?"

Dear One, you are needing to see an endocrinologist. There is an issue in the thyroid and other endocrinology too.

"She said my thyroid numbers are fine."

This is true they are fine numbers. They are not good numbers for you, and you are addicted to sugar. Addicted to that which you think will give you energy and then it robs you blind when you are not looking. You are going towards diabetes and it is a slide down to this without someone smarter about these things than you. You have sufficient insurance and you can choose to see an endocrinologist for yourself. Just see what this doctor has to say. You will find support that you are badly needing. Also this one will help with brain fog. You can't think very good. Yes?

"I can't think clearly at all! I thought I might be getting early dementia."

This difficulty will get resolved when the body is back to balance both the endocrine system as well as structural. You will need chiropractic, Dear One, because you will carry the body differently than you now do. The change of your head as it stands upon the spine needs fixing. This is a specialty to this chiropractor to set the head on the spine properly.

KNOWING YOUR INTUITIVE VOICE

My office is located very close to several universities: UCSD, CSUSM, SDSU, USD, and two city colleges as well. I have the opportunity to see many college students in my practice. This is a time in their life when they are making huge life decisions. Often these decisions are being made before they are able to get in touch with who they really are and what they enjoy in work. It is very rewarding work to help people determine their best career path.

A recent college graduate named Zack came to see me about his career, which he was just unsure about.

Zack asks:

"What should I be doing with my career?"

You are working at a big store. Yes?

"Yes. Costco, but that's not my career. I am a biology major and I just can't seem to find a job. And actually there aren't any positions that I am very interested in."

You have lost your heart for this work, Dear One. You wanted to be a scientist. Yes? You wanted to do research, but you cannot stand to be in the room of whiteness?

"Right, yes, well I do want to do research but not with medicine anyway and not really with chemicals, I guess. Mostly I just can't be in a room all day with no windows and I guess I just hate pretty much everything about it really. But I went to school and I have all this debt and I have no idea how to begin a new career direction. Also can you tell me if I will have a girlfriend soon?"

Your self-esteem is not at its best. You have a love of people and they love you. You are with a girl but not so much, because you only like that she likes you as you are right now. You consider yourself to be less than you should be. Therefore if she will have you now, then you don't think much of her. Crazy yes? Oh well, true anyway. Your relationship will resolve as your work becomes more satisfying. You will not allow yourself to have the relationship of your dreams while you feel unworthy of it.

So for work you are better around people. Your education is good. It is your expectations that may need to adjust a bit. This is not to give up or quit the dreams altogether. You are resistant to the idea of giving up. We think of this not as giving up, but rather, to make a new decision.

This new decision might be: I want to be outside more of the time. I want to be around people and I need variety. You love the idea of research but not a job that involves only doing research. Make a decision to choose what makes you happy in all things. Research online the kinds of jobs there are for people with a biomedical degree. We recommend to try sales of medicine, pharmaceutical sales is a better fit for you, Dear One.

Write down things you want in your career and how you want to feel doing the job. Research how athletes use visioning to create the outcome they want. Practice this for attracting the job you feel good doing.

You will need to set up new goals. This will seem to overwhelm you until you make small lists that will be the path to the larger goal. The big goal of career change will excite you when you believe it is achievable.

Beth has known Larry for a long time. They dated in high school, but they both ended up marrying other people after high school. As time passed, one became a widow, while the other got divorced.

They found each other again when they were both single. Now they have been married for seven years. Beth knows that Larry is who she wants to spend her life with. Here is the problem and question Beth presented to Spirit.

"My marriage is very unhappy, but I know we love each other and both want to stay together. Do you have anything you can tell me that will help my marriage?"

Yes, Dear One. You are very clear on what you want, and this is the best to start with. You also know he wants to be happy in this marriage; this too is a great beginning. There has been much hurt both ways and you need to resolve some past issues. Right now you are stuck each clutching onto how bad the situation for you has been. You are acting like separate teams, and in a team divided, you will both lose. You must unite against the "who done it" and the "how bad it was" and stop blaming each other. The people you are blaming have changed and you are still further able to change. This would be similar to holding a grudge against your five- and six-year-old children for soiling the pants at two years old. You don't need to forgive the kids, because there is nothing to forgive. They simply have grown up and are no longer those same kids and their mistakes will be new ones as they continue to grow. You have to want the marriage more than you want to be right. More than you want him to be wrong. Same truth goes for him.

You have to want the marriage more than you want to be right.

KNOWING YOUR INTUITIVE VOICE

Beth has now written down her goal: "Perfect Marriage Partnership."

She has also made a list of several changes she believes will support her goal.

- Get rid of toxic friends.
- Get involved with our church and our friendships there.
- Start building friendships that share our values and with happily married couples.
- Find a good marriage counselor.
- No more venting to friends and family, talking bad about each other EVER to others.
- Make a list of our part in the breakdown.
- Read books on forgiveness.
- List all the qualities we love in each other.
- Treat this relationship as my most treasured possession and defend it at all cost.

Enjoy the process of getting to the center of the things that matter most. Set your goals and get all areas of your life into balance. Don't accept anything less. You deserve to have it all! It is totally achievable to arrive at that juicy center of your perfectly balanced life.

To have a completely balanced life and achieve your goals, your home needs to support you. We each have a particular environment in which we thrive. Learn what yours is and create a personal space that supports your needs. My home must be a harmonious, loving, balanced and peaceful place in order for me to function at my best. I also enjoy friends and entertaining so my home has an energy that invites fun and playfulness.

Creating a home that supports all of your goals is important, but understanding what your home says about you can also give great insights. When it comes to your home, this is what your living space represents. Your upstairs represents your private life, and private thoughts. The downstairs represents what you want the world to see of you, your personality and worldly desires. The visible home is your public person. The house you can see is just that, your image that people can see.

The cupboards and closets represent your mind and spiritual well-being. Are the cupboards and closets crammed with confusion? Maybe they are disorganized and overflowing, from stuffing things away, so that your outer world can look perfect? Some people are meticulous about folding, stacking and organized cupboards (organized mind), but let the outside get chaotic.

Whether you like your home neat and tidy or looking lived in does not matter as long as it is supporting the lifestyle you desire. Create whatever gives you peace and supports a happy life. I have been invited to many homes to bring peace through Feng Shui. Most homes will be improved greatly just by removing the clutter. Removing clutter from our home is a constant pursuit. I will say that minimizing your "stuff," as in clutter, can help you minimize your "stuff," as in hang ups.

The life of a minimalist can be more peaceful and calming. It is also true that too strict of adherence to perfection can represent an extreme need for control over life. The more confusing things are around the house the harder it is to think, find things, and function.

For myself being highly intuitive and out with Spirit much of my day, you could say I am sometimes not grounded. This can pose a problem for me because when it comes time to get out the door, packed, and ready, I sometimes have a bit of trouble. (This is an understatement according to my family.) I find that a place for everything and everything in its place helps me a great deal but does not come naturally to me. I keep observing people who are organized and then I copy what they do.

I need routine to keep an ordered life, but I am not a routine kind of person. I am blessed to have a partner in life who is organized and has his feet on the ground. I function best with a schedule and routine. But I rebel against schedules and routine. I read a lot about organization and have developed some knowledge in this area, through practice.

It is just as important to ask what must I do away with?

If you are a little scattered or too much "stuff" has accumulated, consider hiring an organizer to help you catch up and to set some routines for you. I have a very good organizer to help me from time to time. She is a big help; it is what she specializes in and she is naturally gifted at organization. She sees things in a way I just don't see them. I know that when things are messy they get messier. I call it the Law of Messy. Reducing possessions does help.

It feels so good to pack up your extras and cast offs for donation. I enjoy knowing someone in need will be able to enjoy the things we no longer need.

When you set new goals for love, home, and career you may find yourself moving into new spaces. When you move into new offices or homes it is very helpful to clear out the energy of the past. Any home can benefit from an energetic cleansing and it becomes absolutely necessary following any traumatic events in your personal environment. When you move into a new home or office you surely don't want to take on the energy of the previous inhabitant. You probably don't wish to inherit the energy or live in the energy left behind such as anger, depression, personality conflicts, etc. Especially if the previous inhabitant has vacated because of divorce, death, or trauma of any kind. There are techniques you can use to clear or remove the energy of the previous inhabitants. No matter how wonderful the previous inhabitant may have been, you want the energy of your space to be purely your own. Think about clothing, and in this case you would always wash clothing before you wear it. In any space you move into the tendency is to give it a once over cleaning even if it has already been cleaned. You would be wise to wash the space of any energy left by the previous tenant, before you move in.

You also want to use this opportunity to set up a great energy for happiness, success, and all of your dreams. Each room from the dining room and kitchen to the master and guest rooms all have a purpose. Be sure to declare the purpose you would like each room to fulfill. This is easily done simply by standing in the room and speaking your intention for this room. Then make sure the furniture and decor match your intentions. If you will be painting the room, this is a fabulous opportunity to write your intention on the wall in pencil. Go ahead and write all kinds of great intentions. Write them big and have fun. It will be painted over and unseen by everyone but you, and it will remain an active manifesting tool in bringing the energy you want into the room. Similar results can be achieved by setting your intention for a room or furniture and by placing a written intention on the underside of any object.

When it comes to the use of a room it is beneficial to think about what you will be using a room for. If you want the master bedroom to be a place of love and sensuality that is enough of a job for one room, especially a room that can define the mood of the entire house. A happy couple makes a happy home. For example, it is not a good idea or very peaceful to have an office or gym space in the master bedroom unless perhaps that is all you want to accomplish in that room. If you are feeling romantic, a sure way to kill the mood would be to walk into an office space and be thinking of all the work you should be doing.

You have really killed the mood if you see the unused gym equipment in your view as you take your lover to bed, unless of course that sort of thing makes you both think how fit, beautiful and sexy you are. Perhaps you will enjoy yourself and your partner more by being in the present activities rather than thinking, "Gee, I should have been working out lately."

If you have a room that must serve dual purposes, and you cannot think of an alternative arrangement, the rooms can be energetically defined as separate. This might be done by using a folding screen or plants or even furniture.

These are my practices for clearing energy to create an environment of peace and tranquility.

Throw open all the windows and doors, draperies and cabinets. Burn sage or incense to clear the old energy. Burning sage can smell like marijuana and you might have concerns about your neighbors or coworkers. :) I find incense works equally well. Use three sticks of incense to symbolize the Trinity. The Trinity can be described in several different ways, i.e.: Father, Son, and Holy Ghost; Body, Mind, and Spirit; Burning the incense or sage walking through the entire house, run the smoke along the base of the wall from the floorboards and letting it travel up the wall. Scoop a bit of smoke into each space, cupboard or cabinet, the entire perimeter of each room and closet. As you go through your home or office it is very important the intention you carry with you. Control your thinking, you are not "ridding" yourself of someone or something so much as releasing. Bless this space with Holy Spirit and with Love. It is very helpful to chant or sing as you complete this clearing, as it will help the mind and intentions to stay focused. A perfect chant for you might be "Negative Energy Goes—Positive Energy Flows" or " I release and I let go—I let love flow." Another good clearing chant is " I release (insert name) from this space with ease and grace."

Your space is clean and ready for your intentions and blessing. If it is an office space, your new intention might be success, respect, friendship, great customer relations and great income.

The Blessing can be as simple as standing in the room and saying a prayer as to your intentions for the room. A bell or chime that is pretty to the ear can be helpful to establish and ring in your intentions. I use a bell from Tibet, a gong, and sometimes a ceremonial drum depending on my inner guidance.

By now you have identified what needs to be added or deleted from your life to create balance. You have set your goals and started making some needed changes. You have begun your meditation practice. The next key to living a life Divine will be to understand and trust your intuitive voice. By now I hope you realize that your intuitive voice is the wisdom of God guiding your life in perfect harmony.

Intuition is not something you do. Intuition is a way in which you live. I live what I would call a Spirit-led life. By this I mean that Spirit or God leads me, I don't try to lead my life. Believe me, I like to be in control as much as anyone. I have learned over the years that when I surrender to a higher source the outcome is always better than I could have imagined. I no longer try to be in control of my will. I have a will, you can be sure of that. I make God laugh all the time by telling him/her what I have in mind for this or that. I experience my desires and free will fully. I then ask for guidance from God and choose to follow God's Will over my own.

This is one of my daily prayers that I have said for thirty years, maybe more:

> *"Thy Will be done in and through me, and my life, for the highest and best good of all."*

Surrendering to a higher wisdom, a higher will, has transformed the way I live my life.

KNOWING YOUR INTUITIVE VOICE

I still have a mind of my own that percolates with ideas and dreams. These combine with the intuition that comes along as well. I get tons of ideas and feel excited and motivated by many inclinations. Of course I express those in my conversations with God. Then I always ask, "Thy Will be done in and through me and my life for the highest and best good of all." Then I wait for a sign or message that lets me know the direction to go forward.

I prefer prayers of gratitude over prayers of asking. Gratitude works like a vacuum pulling more of the good things you are grateful for into your life. Gratitude is an emotion and anytime you get in touch with emotion you are in touch with a manifesting energy.

It can be difficult controlling the negative thoughts when we feel emotionally connected to them. When you are telling the story of "how bad it was" you have a tendency to really get into convincing the person you're sharing with and you probably find you are quite emotionally involved in the story. If it was not impactful you would probably not even bother to share the story in the first place. Be careful because you are in manifesting energy when you are telling and retelling an emotional story whether it is a positive or negative experience.

I keep a Gratitude journal. Every evening I write down several things, people, and experiences that I am grateful for. I hope you will consider keeping a gratitude journal. When I first began keeping a gratitude journal, I found that my gratefulness increased. I began thinking of things I was grateful for as my day went along. I looked forward to the people, situations and things I would be writing in my gratitude journal. You could say practicing gratitude created more gratitude in me, and also manifested more and more to be grateful for.

This is just one example of a gratitude style of prayer.

"Dear God, Thank you for all our many blessings. Thank you for this food, and for blessing each and every person that made

this food possible at our table. Make this food blessed with thy holy light, helping each one of us to be all that we can be. Thank you for our family and loved ones. Thank you for the blessings of love, health, wealth, and happiness. May all the world know, Thy love and Thy peace."

We always pray from our hearts in a fresh personal conversation with God and nothing canned or memorized.

It can be a bit hard for me to stay grounded. I fell into accounting because math was easy for me. Now I find that I have forgotten most of it. I have found that spending six hours a day gone from my body in trance and meditation has rewired my brain. I am not as linear in my thinking as I once was. I spend no time with numbers and math so that is no longer my greatest strength. I think differently. I am also more scattered, airy perhaps, than I once was. I don't see the benefit of being scattered, but it's my truth, so it seems only fair to share it with you here. I am grateful for the grounded people in my life.

I would like to point out that I experience two types of meditative experiences. When I speak about meditation here I have been speaking strictly about getting connected to God in a deep clear way. I do this every day just to be in communion with God and I do not seek any answers at this time. This is of foremost importance and is what each of us must do in order to develop a clear and beautiful connection with our Divine source.

Being an Intuitive Channel is a unique condition in which I am able to enter a meditative state (also referred to as a trance state) and become an instrument of God. As an intuitive channel I am allowing myself to be used as a voice of Spirit for those who are not yet able to hear clearly for themselves. The meditation I experience when I am channeling is very different and not something I ever intended to do. It has been something that developed out of many years of meditation. Channeling is my calling or dharma in this lifetime and not something that I tried in any way to create.

Seek first to connect with God. In other words seek God in meditation, not answers. Your personal calling will be revealed to you. It will be a perfect fit and a perfect blessing for you. Don't meditate to receive answers. Meditate to receive God and the answers will come. Your intuition will become clear for you.

I try to always be in complete surrender to God's Will for me. The path I have chosen to take in this lifetime, and God has chosen for me, is Divinely written in my astrological chart and the palm of my hand.

I want to be in alignment with my highest and best good. I know Spirit personally, having spent hours per day over the last thirty years in meditation for myself and others. I know there is a wise and wonderful Creator that will guide me in the very best direction for me. I know the same is true for every living creature on the planet. This profound wise guidance is there for you to tune into as well. You need to meditate and practice, and just like any other skill you will get better with repeated efforts.

Even knowing this, I tend to get fretful and worried easily and this is one of my human traits. I have to bring myself back to center. I am a born worrier, a bit of anxiety and nervousness chases me around. I know better, and I catch myself, but it's there in my nature. With practice I hope to diminish my shortcomings and develop my strengths. I believe that is what we are all here for. To do our best. Enjoy our lives, and help to improve the lives of others.

Where do you find freedom from worry, and achieve a peaceful mind? You can't purchase it anywhere. You can't inherit it from Dad or Great Grams either. It is something you need to develop for yourself. Meditation offers freedom from worry, and achieve a peaceful mind, but requires devoted practice. You don't expect to make beautiful music even from the most expensive instrument, without practice. It may help you to adjust your expectations regarding meditation. Although the basics are simple to learn, deep meditation is a developed skill, and requires time, patience, and dedication to master. Don't expect that you will travel time and space and have spectacular awakenings where you know all Truth the first time you attempt meditation. Please do call me right away though, if this happens for you!

What if you could be happy no matter the circumstances of your life? Peace and calm in life brings joy and makes the life worth living. One of the wonderful blessings of meditation is that it creates peace and calm.

Setting up a regular meditation schedule is helpful. It creates a habit and habits are hard to break. This is a great habit to develop. Begin with just two minutes and work up ideally to twenty minutes or more two times per day. Best time for morning meditation is before six a.m. Don't start making excuses for yourself if you do not get up this early, because any time of the day is good for meditation. Regularity is the key. Most people find that morning and evening meditation just before bed and just upon rising in the morning are the easiest commitments to keep, and the easiest habits to form. Once the habit of meditation is formed it is very easy to keep. You will even begin to crave it. Much like some of you may get up and the first thing you think of is coffee. Eventually, you will crave meditation, the same as you crave that morning cup of coffee or your favorite tea. You find you just don't feel right without it. Once you have developed the habit of meditation, your body anticipates meditating at a particular time of day. Your meditation practice becomes much easier to settle into. In fact each time you repeat your habit, the brain creates pathways making habit paths in the brain to make each subsequent meditation easier to enter. A deeper experience will become available with continued practice.

I feel directed to repeat how to meditate, because it is so important. There are many different ways to meditate, so you may wish to research a different style of meditation than I use. I often chant for a while before the deepest part of my meditation. Ultimately I meditate in complete silence. I will explain a slightly different meditation technique this time. Maybe you will gather a small bit of information that you didn't realize in the previous instruction.

- Find a peaceful and quiet place to meditate.
- Back straight, in lotus position or in a straight back chair.
- Palms up, right hand resting in the left, thumbs lightly touching.
- Or palms up resting on the upper thigh.
- Close your eyes and turn them upward to gaze upon the location. of the third eye. The third eye is not a physical eye. It is located in the center of the forehead just above the level of the eyebrows. This is the center that must awaken for intuition.
- Chanting helps many of us to quiet the mind to enter meditation. Chant for as long as you like, silently or out loud.
- Breathe slowly in and out through your nose.
- Become aware of your breathing without trying to control it.
- Pay close attention to the sensation of the breath as it enters and leaves the nostrils.
- Become aware of the cool air entering the nostrils.
- Become aware of the subtle warmth of the breath as it passes out of the nostrils.
- Rest your mind upon your breath.
- Forget all other thoughts and feelings; simply focus on the breath.
- With every inhalation and exhalation observe the gentle motion of your body.
- If your mind wanders onto other thoughts, redirect your attention to the breath.
- With each breath feel yourself relax more deeply.

212

- When you are done meditating release your concentration from the breath.
- As you leave meditation bring out with you the sense of stillness and peace.

When you first try meditation you may find it is hard to quiet the mind. When I first am entering meditation I experience a flow of thoughts coming. Something like being in the middle of a stream or brook that flows like water but is made of spiritual energy. The flow of this energy stream is washing over me and through me. When thoughts come along, it is as if debris is floating in my stream. I find it helpful to experience the thoughts as if they are just floating past me. I am aware of thoughts coming down the river as if they exist in my peripheral vision. I observe that they float by and make no effort to retrieve them. I keep returning to my breath with a calm and settled mind. Sometimes a thought catches my attention and draws me away from my focus upon the breath. When I become aware this has happened, I just release it back into the stream of energy and gently return to my breath. To a persistent distraction, sometimes I will say, inside my mind, "not now, we will talk later, I am meditating now."

There are numerous ways to meditate. Many people find using a repeated mantra helps them to meditate deeply. I first learned to meditate by repeating a mantra or chant. Chanting is the singing of a repeated phrase called a mantra over and over again.

Many mantras are in the very ancient and sacred language of Sanskrit. The word mantra is derived from the Sanskrit word: *Man* meaning "to think" or Manas meaning "Mind" and *Tra* which designates a tool or instrument. Therefore a mantra is a tool, used by the mind that eventually helps us to travel from the mind and frees us from the mind.

The first mantra I learned was, Om Namah Shivaya. It was explained to me as meaning, "I honor God in all that is." A closer interpretation might be "I offer to Siva (God) a respectful invocation of His Name." The actual meaning in this mantra is associated with qualities of prayer, divine love, grace, and truth. Traditionally it is used as a powerful healing mantra beneficial for the clearing of all ailments and blockages. Om is the sound or vibration of every living thing in the universe. Om or AUM acts much like saying Amen, and is a mantra in itself, which means God. Om or AUM is often chanted at the beginning or ending of yoga sessions. Namah in Sanskrit means to give or offer honor, to acknowledge, in this case to Shivaya, a Sanskrit name for God. This mantra has strong spiritual powers.

There are many beautiful chants and mantras. Mantras that are created by Holy Masters and Gurus are fixed with great spiritual power. Because many of these chants have been repeated by so many over thousands of years, they have gained a very strong spiritual power. Holy Masters and teachers are often called Gurus. Guru may be an unfamiliar or uncomfortable word depending on the religion or culture you were raised in. The word guru is another Sanskrit word and simply means "teacher." In the Hindu and Indian culture, however, it means much more than a simple teacher. It means Master Teacher, or Dispeller of Darkness, and represents one that has achieved oneness with God. Christians honor Jesus as God. Many Gurus also regard Jesus as a manifestation of God.

When it comes to mantras, find a phrase that represents your highest vision of greatness in the universe.

You can even choose to repeat a meaningful phrase such as "Love is all there is" or Om Shivaya Om, or Om Jesus Om. Put in any word that gives you comfort as long as it represents your highest honoring of Creator.

I find chanting to be a very peaceful and enjoyable practice that centers me into a deep meditation. Minds seem to want constant movement and chanting can be very helpful in stilling the mind for meditation. Some forms of meditation have you chanting the entire time.

Minds are in constant movement. It is through our minds that we experience our world. We interpret how the world is by our satisfaction with it. The world is a constant whirl of multitasking, with many distracting things happening in this stimulating time on our planet. This can cause us to be restless and unsatisfied. You can eliminate the chaos of the mind and experience inner peace and comfort with meditation.

We all have extremely busy lives. We need time for a mini time out. Have you ever wished the world would stop spinning for just a moment, and you could temporarily step off and relax? Well, you can, and it's called meditation.

Do you wish you didn't worry about making the wrong decision? Do you sometimes feel stuck or crippled with indecision? Meditation brings peace and calm to your rescue and improves intuition.

When the turbulence of a crazy world has you swirling in the spin cycle, intuition can help you to cope with and settle the confusion. So much of our pain and suffering is caused or aggravated by our stress. Fear of the unknown and making wrong decisions cause a great deal of stress. Through intuition, difficult situations become easier to deal with and all relationships become more peaceful and satisfying. Our relationships improve, decisions come easier, our stress reduces.

We all want peaceful and enjoyable relationships with our partner, family, coworkers and friends. We want peace between countries. What prevents us from having satisfying relationships? Our approach to others cannot come from what's in it for me or how can this person make me happy. We need to be thinking—what can I do to understand them better? What do they need from me, so they can find joy and satisfaction in this relationship?

Why is it important to create a peaceful mind? The simple reason is because we want to be happy in all areas of life. The function of meditation is to make the mind peaceful and calm *so that you can know God.*

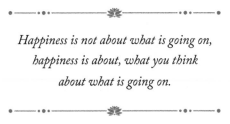

Happiness is not about what is going on,
happiness is about, what you think
about what is going on.

I am grateful for every experience in my life as well as each and every one of the people who played their part in my drama. Yes, I do mean thank you to the villains in my life story. Without you and the experiences you offered, I would not be exactly me. I know I have personal growth yet to take care of, however, where I am right now cannot be fully appreciated and enjoyed unless I embrace all that has brought me to this place.

I hope that you have found something on these pages that gives you peace, guidance, and clarity toward the answers you seek. May you always seek a deeper relationship with Spirit and your personal intuitive voice.

I shared my truth here and shared the Truth that Spirit asked me to share. There is plenty more to discover as you delve deeply into your personal spiritual awakening. Through God and your intuitive voice I know you will have a lifetime of learning the enriching lessons of our universe.

Most of all it is my wish that you feel loved by me and the Divine. May God bless you in every way.

ॐ

Warmest Blessings,

Shawna....the Knowing One

ABOUT THE AUTHOR

Shawna has been a successful business owner for over thirty years. Prior to this she was the accountant for the largest property management and real estate company in Vail, Colorado. As Miss Vail, Colorado, she had the opportunity to interact with and assist such celebrities as President Gerald Ford and First Lady Betty Ford as well as Bob Hope and the cast of *Charlie's Angels* and many others.

Shawna Allard brings over three decades of speaking experience along with her trusted expertise as an Intuitive leader. Born psychic and empathic, she is passionate about teaching and guiding others to understand their personal intuition. She enjoys teaching and inspires people to live their best lives, in body, mind, and spirit.

She is a sought-after speaker, engaging small groups to audiences greater than 300 attendees. Her presentations to large audiences include Chapman University, California State University of San Marcos, National Association of Women Engineers, National Gathering of Holistic Nurses Association, and others. She has appeared on television shows including *The Dr. Dohn Show, Healing Voices* , and *The Parapsychology Show*. She has been a popular guest on local and national radio as well.

Shawna has written several articles in *By The Numbers* and other publications. She is a featured author in the book *Women of Spirit*.

Shawna has served on the governing board of The Orange County Society Of Psychic Research. Has enjoyed membership in The Feng Shui Guild, American Association of Hands on Healers, Women's Wisdom and Holistic Nurses Association.

Shawna supports a variety of Women's organizations including Straight From The Heart, Women's Empowerment, Micro Loans for Women, and Freedom for Victims of Human Trafficking.

She lives in Southern California with her husband and youngest son who is now a senior in high school. She and her husband have been blessed with three wonderful children and one very special son-in-law. Their two oldest children are grown adults successfully navigating career and family here in San Diego. She also has two small and playful dogs that take her for long walks. She enjoys organic gardening, hiking, beach walks, boogie boarding, meditation, yoga, a good book, and the performing arts.

Shawna envisions a future where everyone has a personal relationship with God and understands their personal intuitive voice.

AUTHOR CONTACT INFORMATION

Shawna is available for Intuitive Clairvoyant
and Channeled readings, Spiritual Counseling,
Reiki Healing
and more by appointment only.

Channeled Sessions are offered by phone or in person.

Schedule online:
www.DivineKnowing.com

Schedule by phone:
(800)-KNOWING
(800)-566-9464

Book Website
www.DivineKnowing.com

For a schedule of classes and events
www.DivineKnowing.com

If you are interested in more information please
sign up to receive my email newsletter at
www.DivineKnowing.com

I am delighted to donate a portion of the proceeds
from *Knowing* to this wonderful organization.

The mission of Women's Empowerment International (WE) is
to give women the tools they need to work their way out of poverty.
WE is part of a global movement, that by 2030 aims to eliminate the
poverty of 1.5 billion people who live on $1.90 a day.

WE stands for the 70% of the world's poor who are women.
They struggle to feed their families, provide a safe home, and educate
their children. Most have nowhere to turn.

A San Diego-based international nonprofit, WE has donated
over $1.3 million to fund 25,000 business startup and expansion
loans to poor women in Honduras, Ghana, Benin, Uganda, Haiti and
Mexico, and to help San Diego women launch 300 businesses. All
repaid WE loans are reissued so even a modest gift to WE can start
many businesses.

Women like Muhabbat, whose family of six struggled to live
on $850/month in welfare. With free help from WE's STAR Center
in San Diego, she started a licensed childcare business and in two
months increased her income by 70%.

In Uganda, Kellen lost five of her ten children to AIDS and now
is raising three orphaned grandchildren. With a $17 WE loan, she
bought two piglets. She'll sell two grown pigs for $99, and use the
profits to feed and clothe her grandchildren, buy more piglets and
build a pig pen. All that from a $17 loan.

With an $87 WE loan, Karen busses to the city to buy used clothing she sells from her rural Honduran home. Through two years of tireless work, Karen's loans, inventory, profits and confidence have grown. Now she can afford school for her children—their first step out of poverty.

With even a $100 donation, you can give impoverished women hope, the opportunity to start a business, and the ability to shelter, feed and educate her children. Please give today to Women's Empowerment International. Your donation will change lives.

Donate at
www.womenempowerment.org

or by mail at
Women's Empowerment International
PO Box 501406, San Diego, CA 92150-1406
(619) 333-0026.

WE is a 501(c)(3) nonprofit;
donations are tax-deductible.